Welcome

This is one of 133 itinerary-based *Pocket Guides* produced by the editors of Insight Guides, whose books have set the standard for visual travel guides since 1970. With top-quality photography and authoritative recommendations, this guidebook is designed to help visitors get the most out of Melbourne and its surroundings during a short stay.

To this end, it brings you the best of the city and its surroundings in 15 itineraries devised by Insight's correspondent, Cameron Duffy. It begins with three full-day tours linking the essential sights, the first exploring the area south of Bourke Street, the second Melbourne's best beachside suburb, St Kilda, and the third focusing on the inner city arts precinct and recent riverside development, Southgate. These are followed by 10 shorter tours, exploring other interesting areas and aspects of the city, and two excursions, the first to the wineries of the Yarra Valley and into the bush of the Dandenong Ranges, and the second to Victoria's second largest city, Geelong, and along the Great Ocean Road. Each itinerary includes ideas on where to lunch or dine on the way. The itineraries are supported by sections on history and culture, eating out, shopping and nightlife (including recommended venues), plus a calendar of special events. At the end of the guide is a detailed practical information section covering transport, money matters, communications, etc, and a list of recommended hotels at all price levels.

Cameron Duffy is a former Insight editor, who was based in the company's London office. He lived and worked as a reporter, writer and editor in London for seven years before Australia beckoned him home. He delights in the beauty and bohemian nature of his home city, understanding why it continues to top lists of the world's most livable cities. In preparing this Pocket Guide to Melbourne his aim has been to give the visitor a real feel for the city. He pays due attention to the must-see sights, the beachside suburb of St Kilda and historic Williamstown, and explores the best of the inner-city area. But he is also keen to introduce the visitor to the wonderful bars, restaurants and cafés that Melbourne has to offer. He says, 'the city's friendly residents will make sure the enlightenment isn't just culinary'.

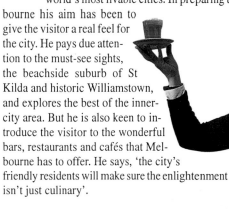

introduction

HISTORY AND CULTURE

CITY ITINERARIES

The city itineraries link Melbourne's best sights in order of priority. The first three are designed for visitors with only three days in the city, giving a mixture of inner-city sights, the arts precinct and a beachside suburb. The next 10 explore other interesting areas.

INSIGHT

Leabhar Chontae Luimni

MELBOURNE

APA PUBLICATIONS
Part of the Langenscheidt Publishing Group

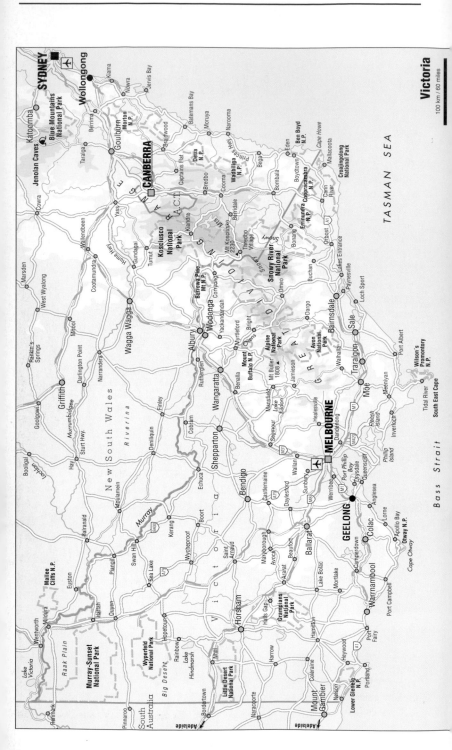

Victoria

100 km / 60 miles

contents

EXCURSIONS

Two excursions to destinations within easy reach.

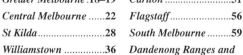

LEISURE ACTIVITIES

CALENDAR OF EVENTS

PRACTICAL INFORMATION

MAPS

CREDITS AND INDEX

Page 1: Collingwood supporter. **Pages 2/3**: Federation Square
Pages 8/9: the city from the Yarra River

History & Culture

Over the years, Melbourne and its citizens have drawn a fair amount of both criticism and praise. In the early 20th century, when Ellen and Henry Kean were performing *Richard III*, Ellen wrote to their son: 'They know no more how to appreciate your father's acting than how to write a Greek epigram...Fifth rate talent is good enough for them. They are incapable of distinguishing the delicacies of art.' Half a century later Ava Gardner, star of the 1959 film *On the Beach*, shot in Melbourne, said the city was the perfect place to make a film about the end of the world.

Another member of the acting profession, H.M. Hyndman, writing in 1911, had a far higher opinion of the city: 'I have been a great deal about the world and I have moved freely in many societies, but I have never lived in any city where the people at large, as well as the educated class, took so keen an interest in all the activities of human life, as in Melbourne at the time I visited it. Art, drama, music, literature, journalism, wit, oratory, all found ready appreciation. The life and vivacity of the place were astonishing. It's only drawback was rather neatly expressed by the brother of Bernal Osborne. Asked how he liked Melbourne, he replied: "Immensely. But don't you think it's a little far from town".'

Back in the 1860s, George Augustus Sala, a British journalist, had described Melbourne in London's *Daily Telegraph* in even more glowing terms: 'I found Melbourne a really astonishing city with broad streets full of handsome shops and crowded with bustling well-dressed people.' He dubbed the city 'Marvellous Melbourne', saying it was 'teeming with wealth and humanity'. He believed the gold-rush period had left behind 'a residuum of "real live men", as the Americans say, and those live men and their sons [had] made Melbourne what she is: magnificent and marvellous.' Today the city regularly features in the top five on lists of the world's most livable cities. It is something that its citizens are quietly proud of. They don't need a big harbour, an opera house or fancy bridge. Keep it quiet that marvellous Melbourne is a pleasant place to live with just the right mix of residents and visitors, and, with a bit of luck, the city will stay that way.

But perhaps not for long. International visitors to Melbourne have increased by 10 percent per annum in the past few years (to about 135,000 in 1998). And with spin-off visitors from the Sydney Olympics in 2000, as well as fans coming to the Commonwealth Games in 2006, the rise in numbers is expected to continue.

Most first-time European visitors to Australia in 1788, however, had no choice about coming – or leaving. About 1,000 passengers, of which three-quarters were convicts, arrived in Australia that year at Botany Bay, but it was another 40 or so years before Melbourne was settled.

Left: an early impression of an Aboriginal camp
Right: Melbourne's founder, John Batman

The City's Foundation

The first Europeans to arrive found that the Yarra River meandered through a swamp to the west, where waterfowl and fish provided food for the Woiworung Aboriginal people. Here the course of the river turned to the north and east with eucalyptus and large wattles covering slopes on the northern bank. The Yarra opened out into a broad pond backed by a rise of rocks. Near the bottom of what is now William Street, the first Europeans came ashore and grabbed land to establish a trading post. The town's founder, Englishman John Batman, newly arrived from Van Diemen's Land (now Tasmania) bought 240,000 ha (592,800 acres) of land on the shores of Port Phillip and stretching inland, for 30 tomahawks, 40 blankets, 100 knives, 200 handkerchiefs, some flour and a promise of future payments.

This is not to ignore the thousands of years of history in the area: Aborigines had inhabited the region for about 40,000 years – since the Dreamtime, the era that permeates their oral tradition. The Aboriginal population prior to European settlement is estimated at about 300,000, speaking some 500 different languages. Each tribal group, including those around the Port Phillip Bay area of what the Aborigines called Bararing, recognised local landmarks and linked them with the rich mythology of the Dreamtime. As the grounding for all traditional Aboriginal thought and practice, Dreamtime is the Aboriginals' ancestral, cultural and historical heritage.

It wasn't until the 1850s that Melbourne started to come into its own. For the first 12 years of its development it remained part of the colony of New South Wales, administered from Sydney. In its early years Melbourne was pretty well an afterthought. Governors had earlier tried to settle a township elsewhere in Victoria, and the eventual site of Melbourne emerged only from the needs of the agricultural industry.

Melbourne's central grid was laid out in 1837. The lanes between the main streets were originally intended to serve the stables and back offices of buildings fronting the major streets, making it unnecessary to break the major footpaths with carriageways to rear service yards. At first these lanes were not given names for fear they would become streets and prevent sufficient flow of air between buildings – as had happened in Sydney. In 1839 Bishop Perry directed that they should be given names: Flinders Lane, Lonsdale Lane, and so on, but they were never to be recognised as proper streets. He was too late: people not only began to build on the lanes, but demanded access to their rear yards, which meant constructing further lanes. The lanes soon became official streets, and manufacturers and industrialists began to establish offices and warehouses as well as residential buildings. Speculators then subdivided large

Above: the early days of settlement
Right: mail day in mid-19th-century Melbourne

blocks into smaller ones. New retail, recreational, industrial and residential frontages sprang up on these low-cost sites, in some cases creating open arcades between major thoroughfares.

The Gold Rush Years

The early 1840s was a period of severe recession. The municipality of Melbourne was created in 1842 and was granted city status in 1848. But the 1850s saw massive growth following the discovery of gold in Bendigo, Ballarat, Castlemaine, Warrandyte and scores of other places in Victoria. Within two months of becoming officially independent, Victoria was producing more gold than anywhere else in the world.

Melbourne's population increased at a massive rate: from 77,500 people in 1850 to 95,000 the following year. In 1854 about 270,000 immigrants poured into the city (although many did not stay) and by the end of the decade the population had reached half a million. The most important traces of this rapid increase today lie in the physical layout of the city – the central grid, the sites of the public buildings and the arterial routes and approaches. Melbourne's first houses, stores and government buildings were located in the area known today as William Street.

At the time of Melbourne's first land sales, William Street had been planned as the city's premier promenade because it marked the furthest point of the Yarra River that could be reached by ocean craft. It was initially envisaged that this main thoroughfare would extend up from the original crude wharves and alongside the city's first customs house. But then the first punt crossed the Yarra, and in 1854 a bridge was built, connecting Swanston Street to the south, and William Street was established as the southern gateway to the burgeoning town and a direct route to the developing southern areas.

Swanston Street, now the main one in Melbourne, took its name from Charles Swanston, an influential banker in Hobart and a member of the Port Phillip Association. Before long Swanston Street became the busiest north–south thoroughfare in Melbourne and its status was confirmed by the establishment of Flinders Street Station, the Town Hall, the Anglican Cathedral, the Museum and State Library, the Working Men's College (later the Royal Melbourne Institute of Technology), the City Baths and, in the distance to the north, the University of Melbourne.

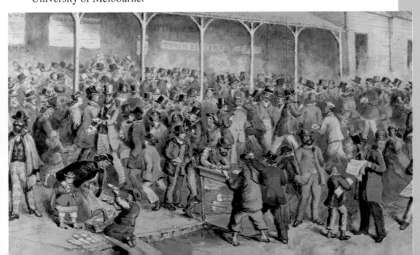

Around this time Eastern Hill and the Parliamentary Precinct were conceived by Charles Joseph La Trobe, the first superintendent of the Colony of Port Phillip and later the Governor of Victoria (in 1839). La Trobe's task was to preside over the subdivision, sale, public allocation and distribution of what was probably the most precious resource in the colony – land. La Trobe's vision resulted in a framework for a genteel city, comprised of well-planned parks, boulevards, government precincts and planned zones where hospitals, offices and shops were built.

La Trobe's plan for the city was set in train without pressure from developers and before the frenzy of the gold rush. Eastern Hill reaped the benefits, which resulted in a harmonious mixture of residential, government and institutional buildings on the edge of the central district.

Some other building and development took place during the gold rush years of 1852–59. Melbourne at this time was a ramshackle, hastily put together place. It was said: 'its streets swarmed with unshaven chins and negligent attire'. In 1853 one new arrival noted that the city had 'the noise and confusion of a second Babel'. The later 1850s, however, were a difficult time, when the boom collapsed, wages fell and changes were made to the economy. The population at this time was still mainly of British stock, with about 110,000 moving here from other Australian ports. About 20,000 were from China and other places, including Germany, Italy and America.

Marvellous Melbourne

Melbourne functioned as a port, a capital and a communications centre, but it was not until the 1860s that great prosperity came to the city, when it managed to take Sydney's title as the financial capital of Australia. The city saw itself as one of the most progressive in the world, and dignified warehouses and dazzling office blocks still survive in west Melbourne from this period. Many of the city's magnificent churches were also constructed during these prosperous years. As migrants rushed to Victoria in search of fortunes, the church responded to their need for spiritual fulfilment. The network of roads, river craft and railways improved communications, and the advent of telegraph services, telephones, electric lights and rapid printing presses spread the civilising influences of the colonial powers throughout the territories.

This was a period when the city was known as

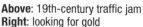

Above: 19th-century traffic jam
Right: looking for gold

'Marvellous Melbourne'. George Augustus Sala had used the phrase repeatedly in his articles in London's *Daily Telegraph*. His reputation gave it authority and it came to be used by residents and promoters of the city. The prosperity was due to the steady rise in technological progress, factory production, tariff protection and urban culture. Manufacturing never dominated Melbourne as it did the cities of industrial Britain. The city grew, in the first instance, out of agriculture and mining, and subsequently from extractive industries, such as brewing and flour milling.

Decline and Revival

The boom was not to last forever. Melbourne entered one of its worst depressions in the 1890s. Appalling droughts and strikes added to the citizens' woes. But good news was just around the corner – in 1901 a federation of the six Australian colonies was achieved and Melbourne served as the nation's capital until Canberra was founded in 1927. The first Federal Parliament opened in the Royal Exhibition Buildings, and in 1906 the Melbourne Symphony Orchestra was formed. It was during this period that Melbourne gradually adopted a more conservative character than its sister Sydney. While Melbourne turned towards subtle European styles, Sydney took on a more racy, American feel.

Many people believe this still applies today, with residents agreeing that 'Sydnesiders will throw a party while Melburnians will give a dinner party.' Perhaps this is also why Melbourne residents are known for wearing black, the colour of laid-back bohemian chic. When making interstate visits, Melburnians are accused of dressing too often in 'Melbourne black'. But it is a tag they are happy to wear. They wouldn't dream of wearing the garish colours seen on the streets of Sydney or on the beaches in Queensland.

As Melbourne entered the 1930s, depression struck again with unemployment peaking at around 30 percent in 1932. In 1933 Melbourne's population passed the one million mark and economic conditions began to improve again. Australia's role in World War II had no dramatic effect on central Melbourne, although in 1942 hundreds of diggers excavated trenches in the parks and gardens in anticipation of air raids.

Above: cable trams on Collins Street in the early 20th century

The City Today

After the war Australia started an ambitious immigration programme with migrants first drawn from the Mediterranean and Baltic countries of Europe and then, in the 1970s, from around the world. The eyes of the world were on Melbourne in the 1950s – with Queen Elizabeth's first visit in 1954, and the Olympic Games, held for the first time in the southern hemisphere in 1956. It was known as the 'friendly games' and, according to the overseas press, Melbourne's citizens lived up to the spirit of the name. Larry Montague wrote in Britain's *Manchester Guardian*: 'Citizens in the streets could not have been pleasanter or more helpful. The Victorian police have been a notable example of stamina, kindliness to the foreign sinners against local laws and general courtesy.'

The 1960s and 1970s were decades of immigration, when Australia opened its doors to the rest of the world. Today Melbourne is believed to be the third-largest Greek city (after Athens and Thessaloniki); is said to have more Maltese (second and third generation) than Malta itself, and large Italian and Southeast Asian populations. The 1980s saw Melbourne accept and embrace these immigrants and all they brought with them – most of all their food. Melbourne is the food capital of Australia. Old Australian cuisine has been brought up to date with a fusion of Asian and Western ingredients to create 'Modern Australian' cuisine. The eclecticism, allied to the Australian readiness to experiment with new tastes and food combinations, has transformed Melbourne cooking.

Bigger, Bolder, Brassier?

In 1992, the state elected a conservative government led by Jeff Kennett, a former advertising executive. Kennett began a programme of aggressive cost-cutting and privatisations, and diverted money into huge civil projects, including Southgate, the Melbourne Exhibition Centre and casino (amid great controversy), the new Museum of Victoria and Federation Square. But by 1999, Kennett was seen as increasingly remote and arrogant, and Steve Bracks, head of the Labor Party, was elected as the new Premier of Victoria. Bracks takes a more consensus-based approach in a fiscally prudent government.

SOUVENIR PROGRAMME
OLYMPIC GAMES
MELBOURNE
AUSTRALIA . 22 Nov-8 Dec . 1956
PRICE ONE SHILLING

That said, new developments continue apace, with the latest ongoing project being the Docklands area in the west. Melbourne is a changing city, its 19th-century architectural heritage complemented by dynamic new buildings and a renewed confidence in the future.

Left: souvenir from the 1956 Olympics

HISTORY HIGHLIGHTS

1788 First fleet arrives in Sydney Cove, with a cargo of convicts.

1802 John Murray is the first white man to enter the Port Phillip Bay area.

1834 John Batman makes a treaty with the Aborigines for 240,000 ha (592,800 acres) of land on Port Phillip's shores.

1837 Robert Hoddle plans the Melbourne central grid system.

1839 Melbourne's first governor, Charles La Trobe, arrives.

1842 The municipality of Melbourne is created.

1848 Melbourne is granted city status.

1850 Melbourne is separated from New South Wales.

1851 Gold is discovered at Buninyong, near Ballarat, and the gold rush begins.

1853 The University of Melbourne is established.

1854 Battle known as the Eureka Stockade, between state troopers and miners protesting against licence fees, takes place at Ballarat.

1860 Population reaches 140,000 and the city enters a period when it is known as 'Marvellous Melbourne'.

1861 First Melbourne Cup horse race, watched by 4,000 people.

1880 The notorious bushranger Ned Kelly is captured in Glenrowan and hanged in Melbourne. The International Exhibition is held in the city.

1888 Great Centennial Exhibition takes place in Melbourne.

1901 Federation of the six colonies becomes the Commonwealth of Australia. Melbourne is made the capital.

1906 Melbourne Symphony Orchestra is formed.

1908 Construction of Flinders Street Railway Station.

1929 Melbourne enters an economic depression.

1933 Melbourne's population passes 1 million mark.

1942 Melbourne becomes Allied headquarters for the Southwest Pacific in World War II.

1945 Australia embarks on immigration programme; Melbourne attracts migrants from Greece, Italy and Malta.

1954 Queen Elizabeth II visits the city.

1956 Olympic Games are held in Melbourne.

1961 Monash University is opened as the city population passes 2 million.

1966 American President L.B. Johnson visits Melbourne and anti-Vietnam protesters throng the city streets.

1967 The last criminal hanging in Australia takes place in Melbourne. The public outcry is so great that capital punishment is abolished in Victoria.

1970 Vietnam moratoria organised; 70,000 people march in the city.

1972 A freak storm floods the city causing cars to float down Elizabeth Street.

1973 The 'White Australia' policy is overturned and Melbourne sees a huge increase in immigrants from SE Asia.

1987 Seven people are shot dead and 19 injured in Richmond by a 19-year-old former army cadet.

1991 Melbourne Central shopping centre opens in the heart of the city.

1992 Southgate development completed on the south bank of the Yarra River.

1996 The city hosts the Formula One Grand Prix for the first time.

2000 Opening of CityLink freeways. Melbourne and Olympic Parks continue to expand with opening of Vodafone Arena.

2002 Completion of Federation Square development in the city centre.

2003 National Gallery of Victoria (NGV) International opens.

2006 Melbourne hosts Commonwealth Games. Redevelopment of the newly named Southern Cross Station and Melbourne Cricket Ground completed.

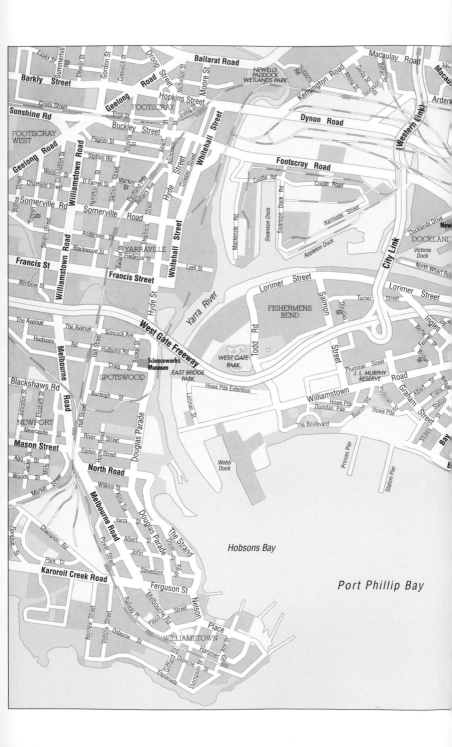

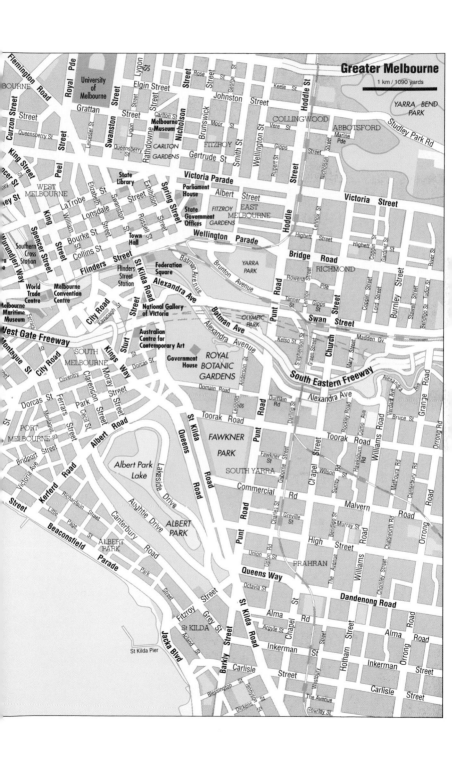

Greater Melbourne

1 km / 1090 yards

OOGIG259

*City
Itineraries*

city itineraries

1. THE CITY GRID – SOUTH OF BOURKE ST *(see map, p22)*

Starting at the grand old Flinders Street Station, this tour works its way through the city grid, including a scenic view from Melbourne's tallest building and a stroll through the financial district, and ending up at Parliament House.

Flinders Street Station is an easy walk for visitors staying in the city; otherwise most public transport connects to the centre.

Melbourne's founders planned the city in a grid-like system *(see page 12)*, which makes it easy to get around. This is helped by the trams, which the city had the good sense to hold onto in the 1950s, when every other major city in the world was abandoning them in favour of buses. The old-style green and gold trams (known as rattlers), which over the decades have become one of Melbourne's most cherished urban icons, are still around but have largely been replaced by newer models. During any part of this tour you can easily jump on a tram running east or west along Flinders or Collins streets.

Start on the corner of Flinders Street and Swanston Street. You can't miss the dramatic architecture of Federation Square, the new iconic development in the heart of the city *(see page 45)*. Swanston Street running north feels like the city's spine – the timeless trams, the grand civic buildings, myriad hip shops and arcades, street art, inspiring churches and, of course, the people who teem in their thousands down this busy boulevard every day.

The city's busiest commuter station, **Flinders Street Station**, is also hard to miss. The imposing bronze-domed building was faithfully restored in 1981 and remains one of Victoria's best-loved public buildings. There is occasional drama and romance as friends and lovers wait for one another on the steps on the corner – a meeting 'under the clocks' has become something of a Melbourne institution. Opposite the station is **Young and Jackson's Hotel**. Built in 1861 on one of the first blocks of land to be sold in Melbourne, the hotel features a famous painting of a nude woman, called *Chloe*, by French artist Jules Lefebvre. Long a subject of fond contemplation and occasional scandal – it was judged indecent at the Melbourne exhibition of 1880 – *Chloe* graces the upstairs restaurant.

On the northeast corner of Swanston Street and Flinders Street stands Melbourne's premier Anglican Cathedral, **St Paul's**. Building began in 1880 after the Church chose English architect William Butterfield to design the building. But Butterfield never even visited Australia, let alone Swanston Street, and eventually resigned from the project due to his dissatisfaction with various modifications to his design.

Left: Flinders Street Station seen from St Paul's Cathedral. **Right**: a city tram

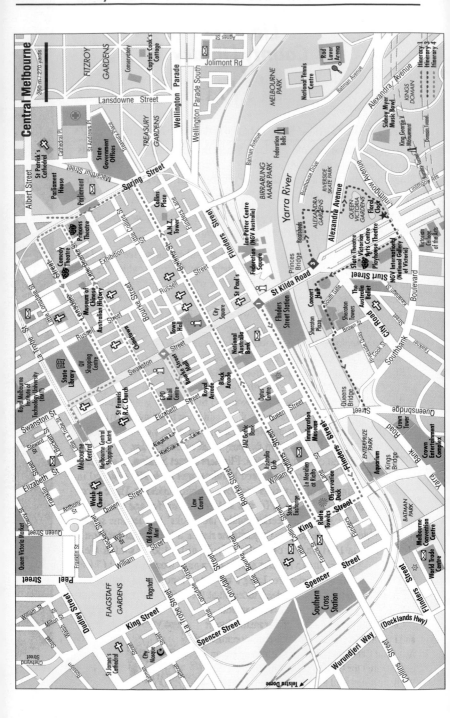

Central Melbourne

The cathedral features three spires added in 1932. Inside, the grandeur created by the vaulted ceiling contrasts with the human scale of other elements and the rich tapestry of colours in the floor and wall tiling.

Leaving the cathedral, walk down Flinders Street past the station, noting the **railway viaduct**. Although it was finished in 1915 the lines were not electrified until 1924. The completion of the city's underground loop had to wait another half a century. Further along Flinders Street, at No. 400, is the **Immigration Museum** (open daily 10am–5pm; closed Good Friday and Christmas Day; tel: 9927 2700; www.immigration.museum.vic.gov.au). The museum brings alive the many experiences of immigration to Victoria since the early 1800s. Nearer the river, on the corner of Flinders Street and King Street, is the **Melbourne Aquarium** (open daily 9.30am–6pm, last admission 5pm; tel: 9620 0999); kids will especially enjoy the transparent tunnel surrounded by sharks and giant stingrays.

Continue in the same direction along Flinders Street, turning right at King Street, past Zanders warehouse. This warehouse, built in 1873, was a result of businesses flushed with trade in the booming 1850s demanding more massive-scale buildings with open internal space.

Collins Street

Turn right at Collins Street and continue to **Rialto Towers**, at 253 metres (823 ft) the tallest office building in the southern hemisphere and a well-known symbol of Melbourne. The observation deck (open daily 10am–late) is worth a visit for the stunning 360-degree views of the city and surroundings. The views extend well beyond the Westgate Bridge to the west, the Dandenong Ranges to the east and the expanse of Port Phillip Bay to the south. The entrance fee also includes the showing of a 20-minute film, *Melbourne the Living City*, which showcases events and attractions in the city and beyond. There's also a café at the top, an ideal place to watch the sunset while enjoying a glass of wine.

The Rialto building located beneath the towers is one of the 19th century Gothic highlights of Collins Street. Redeveloped into a five-star hotel, Le Meridien at Rialto, the

Above: the aquarium logo
Right: view from the Rialto Tower

building has been described as "the quintessential expression of Melbourne's imperial delusions."

Continue walking down Collins Street with the towers behind you. By now you'll be mingling with a swarm of city office workers if it's a weekday. At the intersection of Collins and Queen streets you'll come to the ANZ **Gothic Bank** (open Mon--Fri 9am–4pm; tel: 9273 5555), the former Bank of Australasia. This magnificent Gothic-Revival bank and chambers, designed by William Wardell and completed in 1887, reflects the wealth of 19th-century Melbourne and the vitality of the city's commercial life following the gold-rush boom. It is renowned for the splendour of its interior, which features gold-leaf ornamentation and graceful arches and pillars. Surprisingly, it is still a working bank, which means you can have a good look around during business hours.

Finance and Fantasy Lights

If you look at the buildings which face Queen Street to the north of the bank and Collins Street to the east you will see that they have an identical street facade. These are the entrances to the former **Melbourne Stock Exchange**. Built in 1888–91 and designed in neo-Gothic style by William Pitt, the building features an imposing and richly detailed facade, stained-glass windows, ornate tracery and a fantastic Venetian Gothic tower. Today it houses the ANZ Banking Museum (388 Collins Street; open Mon–Fri 9.30am–4pm; tel: 9273 6831) in the old vault room downstairs from the main entrance.

Further along Collins Street, past Elizabeth Street, is the **Block Arcade**. With its superb mosaic floor and grand period architecture, this is Melbourne's finest and most opulent arcade. Local architect David Askew used the Galleria Vittorio in Milan as his model. You will notice the massive central dome with sculptured supports and the impressive etched-glass roof. The arcade's name derives from the fact that the 'block' sandwiched between Swanston and Elizabeth streets, on Collins Street, was the fashionable place for Melbourne society to promenade during the 1890s. Crossing Elizabeth Street you re-enter the city's shopping precinct. Many of the cafés, restaurants and bars in this area cater mainly for daytime trade. The Australia on Collins and Collins two3four shopping centres are also located here.

Crossing the city's main road, Swanston Street, you will see the **Melbourne Town Hall** (tours Mon–Fri 11am and 1pm, first Sat of the month 11am, noon, 1pm; call first to book, tel: 9658 9658) on your left side, completed in 1870. Inside are some impressive chandeliers and murals, a wood-panelled council chamber and a grand organ, one of the largest in the southern hemisphere. The hall plays host to theatrical performances, wed-

Above: the Rialto Tower, with Le Meridien at Rialto in the foreground
Above right: Block Arcade. **Right:** the Doric columns of Parliament House

dings, receptions and exhibitions. The portico was added in 1887 and has seen many famous visitors to the city, from British royalty to the Beatles.

Opposite the Town Hall is City Square. Cleared of its 19th-century buildings in the 1970s, it underwent a number of transformations before finally coming back to life. During holiday times and lunchtimes you will often find entertainers performing here. A 200-room five-star hotel stands at the back of the square.

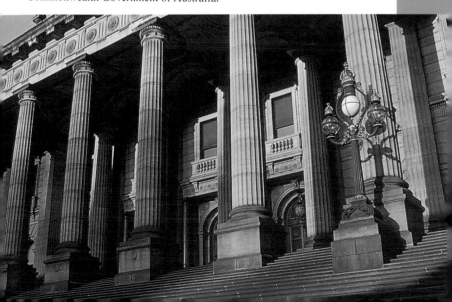

Continuing in the same direction along Collins Street you will come to what tourist offices and city planners have dubbed the Paris end of the street. The somewhat tenuous connection is probably due to the wide tree-lined streets and exclusive continental designer boutiques; the fantasy lights which illuminate the area at night are impressive. This is the heartland of the city's most prestigious street, and it features a mixture of 19th-century architecture, inter-war buildings and more recent office blocks, banks and shops.

At the top end of Collins Street is the **Old Treasury Building** (open daily 9am–5pm), now the city museum. Regarded as one of Australia's finest public buildings, it was designed by a 19-year-old architect, J.J. Clark, and reflects the vision that Melburnians of the 1850s gold-rush era had for their city. The iron lamps and the balustrade at street level add to the building's elegance.

Parliament House

Leaving the treasury building, turn left along Spring Street until you come to **Parliament House** (no tours, but you can go into the public gallery when it's in session). With its sweeping front steps, majestic Doric columns and Italian Renaissance balustrade, Parliament House cuts an impressive figure from its vantage point at the top end of Bourke Street, on what was the high point of the early Port Phillip settlement. Constructed with gold-rush wealth, it has served as the seat of State Government and housed the first Commonwealth Government of Australia.

In July 1851, just weeks before the onset of Victoria's gold rush, the Port Phillip settlement separated from the colony of New South Wales to become the independent colony of Victoria. Some historians argue that, had the separation occurred any later than this, then New South Wales might have been reluctant to lose the enormous income generated by the gold rush, and Melbourne's government precinct would be substantially smaller than it is today.

Upon Federation in 1901, the State Government relinquished the Parliament House to the new Commonwealth Government until the Canberra Parliament House was completed in 1927.

Adjoining Parliament House are **Parliament Gardens**, which make a pleasant spot to finish this tour. Or you might prefer to end the day at the Hard Rock Café at the top of Bourke Street. The restaurant's prices are a little lower than in its London or New York counterparts, but you could be in any Hard Rock Café in the world.

2. ST KILDA *(see map, p28)*

A tour of Melbourne's best-known beachside suburb, St Kilda, which has shed its seedy image to become a hip place to hang out, with great bars, cafés and restaurants.

To get to St Kilda hop on tram Nos. 12, 16 or 96 from the city centre. The starting point is an easy walk from any tram stop in St Kilda.

St Kilda is enjoying a resurgence in popularity, and it's not hard to see why. With its picturesque bayside setting, its proximity to Melbourne and its beaches, restaurants and café lifestyle, it makes a pleasant change from the busy city. St Kilda used to be best known for drugs and prostitution, integral to the area since the 1940s when American servicemen lived here. The prostitutes and drug addicts have largely been pushed out by the rapidly rising cost of real estate, and St Kilda is now more reminiscent of it heyday in the first half of the 20th century when it was a fashionable suburb.

This tour starts at the **Jewish Museum** (26 Alma Road; open Tues, Wed, Thur 10am–4pm, Sun 11am–5pm; tel: 9534 0083; www.jewishmuseum.com.au), a fitting place to start in an area known for its tolerance. The museum features a well-presented timeline – a journey through 4,000 years of Jewish history, and there's an **Australian Jewish History Gallery** which gives an antipodean perspective.

Leaving the museum, continue from Alma Road down Princes Street, and turn left down Fitzroy Street. Formerly dubbed 'Melbourne Terrace', Fitzroy Street was once a centre of prostitution. Since the late 1980s the area has

Above: Hard Rock Café. **Left:** skating in St Kilda
Right: fun on St Kilda beach

been cleaned up and now many of the street workers ply their trade from legal brothels. Buildings such as the George Hotel and Seaview – now a restaurant – a cinema complex, apartments and shops, were also renovated, giving new life to the area. The refurbished Prince (tel: 9536 1122), on the corner with Acland Street, is a prime music venue, and also offers hotel accommodation, a spa retreat and fine dining in its restaurants.

Fitzroy Street is full of groovy bars, cafés and restaurants – a new one seems to open almost every week. Although it's hard to pick a bad one, locals frequent Topolino's at No. 87 for good-value pizza and pasta, or Bar Santo at No. 7 for Mediterranean-style food and a chic ambience.

St Kilda Pier

St Kilda Pier has been successfully rebuilt following a fire in September 2003, which destroyed the kiosk (pavilion) at the end. Residents and the wider community, keen to preserve St Kilda's heritage, ensured the Melbourne landmark was faithfully restored to the original designs of 1904. A modern, yet unobtrusive café has been added to the rear.

Lying a few metres from the St Kilda Pier, a reconstruction of the Lady of St Kilda shipwreck, acquired as a sculptural piece for the 2006 Commonwealth Games, provides an impressive contrast to the urban beach. Leaving from the pier, Melbourne Fishing Charters organise personalised fishing trips catering to experts and novices alike, with special packages also available (tel: 98822061, www.melbournefishing.com; trips depart 7am, 12.30pm and 5pm). Nearby, Yachtpro at the Royal Melbourne Yacht Squadron offers sailing courses for beginners and hires out equipment to experienced sailors. This club house has long been a centre of local sea and land life.

Near the pier are the St Kilda Sea Baths, part of the Melbourne community since the 1850s and now newly restored. Mixed bathing, long a controversial practice, came to be accepted in the area around 1910. Now this quintessentially urban beach is a weekend mecca for visitors and locals, from cyclists and rollerbladers to windsurfers and kiteboarders. It is usually easy to pick the Australians from the foreigners: the Aussies are the ones sitting in the shade, with a broad hat, sunglasses and covered in sunscreen while the rest are baking themselves in the sun. If you need

refreshment now, try the Stokehouse Restaurant (30 Jacka Boulevard, tel: 9525 5555); you can have lunch upstairs and enjoy the magnificent views of Port Phillip Bay and the city skyline.

The Marina

At the south end of the beach is the marina. Watching boats being 'garaged' has become quite a popular pastime here. Sightseers look on as boats – both the small low-priced ones and the luxurious expensive variety – are launched or returned to their racks by giant hydraulic forklift trucks with padded forks.

Coming off the beach, walk straight along Marine Parade and turn left at Dickens Street. Continue straight ahead until you arrive at the **Botanical Gardens** (open daily 7am–4.30pm; 7am–8.30pm during daylight saving time; tel: 9209

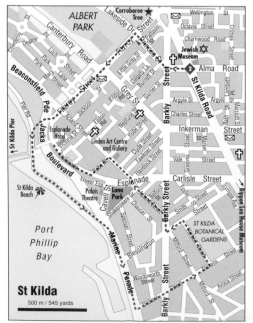

6666), which were laid out on a swamp site. The **Alistair Clark Memorial Rose Garden** contains a major collection of blooms from Australia's most famous rose breeder. The garden was redesigned as a traditional rose garden to coincide with St Kilda's 100th anniversary in 1990. As part of these changes a conservatory was built overlooking a small lake, now home to many birds.

As a possible detour, a short ride on the No. 67 tram, or a 30-minute walk, takes you to 192 Hotham St Elsternwick, site of the **Rippon Lea House**

Above: St Kilda cool

Museum and Historic Garden (open Tues–Sun 10am–5pm; tel: 9523 6095). Rippon Lea is the last of Australia's great privately owned 19th-century suburban estates. Designed and built in 1868 in the Romanesque style, the mansion is surrounded by a beautifully maintained Victorian pleasure ground. The gardens have a host of features, including an orchard, lake, islands and bridges as well as a large Victorian fernery and a conservatory. The 33-room mansion retains much of the lavish decoration favoured by its original owners, and also reflects some of the 1930s Hollywood-style tastes of its last owner.

Leave the Botanical Gardens on the north side, turn left and then right into Barkley Street. Continue until you reach Acland Street on your left. Like Fitzroy Street, Acland Street is full of restaurants, bars and cafés. Part of the street is well known for its delicatessens, continental patisseries and central European cafés and restaurants. The area was a focal point for the wave of European and Jewish refugees who settled in the area during and after World War II. It is now a focal point for tourists, especially backpackers, who come to enjoy the vibrant atmosphere and delicious cakes.

The Esplanade runs off Acland Street. Set high above St Kilda beach it has stunning views of the bay. One of Australia's oldest and longest-running arts and crafts markets is held here every Sunday. Come here for something more original than a stuffed kangaroo.

Luna Park and Linden Gallery

On the corner of the Esplanade and Cavell Street is a long-standing Melbourne icon – the big mouth of an amusement resort called **Luna Park** (open winter: Sat 11am–6pm, Sun 11am–6pm; school and public holidays: Mon–Sun 11am–6pm; summer: Fri 7–11pm, Sat and Sun 11am–6pm; school and public holidays: Mon–Thurs 11am–6pm, Fri 11am–11pm; tel: 9525 5033; www.lunapark.com.au). Opened in 1912, the park underwent a much-needed redevelopment programme in 2001; the park's heritage-listed facades and rides, including the carousel, which dates from 1913, and the dodgems building, from 1926, have been restored to their former glory. The scenic railway, the sole attraction remaining from the park's original opening, is one of the earliest rollercoasters and provides great views over Port Phillip Bay. The latest high-speed thrill rides have been added to bring the park into the 21st century.

Walk back to Acland Street and continue along to the residential area until you come to the **Linden Art Centre and Gallery** (open summer: Tues–Sun 1–6pm; winter: Tues–Sun noon–5pm; tel: 9209 6560; www.lindenarts.org). Housed in a Victorian mansion, built around 1870, the gallery features three exhibition spaces with changing shows.

Leaving the gallery, turn left down Robe Street; now a fashionable street

Right: Rippon Lea House

with fine Edwardian houses, it was once a haunt of prostitutes. Head back towards the Esplanade until you come to the **Palais Theatre** (tel: 9537 244; www.palaistheatre.com). Built in 1913 and then rebuilt in 1927, this splendid building is as much a showpiece as the entertainment it offers. Such greats as Bob Hope, Shirley Bassey, Dame Joan Sutherland and Bob Dylan all appeared here at various times. The foyer's marble columns were beautifully finished by Italian craftsmen.

Continue walking along the Esplanade until you come to the **Esplanade Hotel** (tel: 9534 0211; www.espy.com.au) or simply 'the Espy' as locals call it. Probably Melbourne's best-known pub, the grand building, constructed in 1880, is the live music and performance centre of St Kilda. Saved from redevelopment, this is the perfect place to finish this tour with a glass of wine or a beer.

3. SOUTHBANK AND THE ARTS PRECINCT *(see map, p22)*

Beginning with the peace of the riverside gardens, this tour moves on to NGV International, the cultural heart of the arts precinct, and ends with some retail therapy at the Southgate complex.

The starting point for this tour, the Queen Victoria Gardens, is just across Princes Bridge, which adjoins Flinders Street Station.

Southbank is a vibrant area set alongside the Yarra River, with great views of the city skyline. It is home to many of the cultural mainstays of the city, such as the Victorian Arts Centre, the National Gallery of Victoria (NGV) International and the Melbourne Concert Hall. Alexandra and Queen Victoria Gardens opposite, providing relative calm, are a good place to start.

Alexandra Gardens, sitting on a bend in the River Yarra, are pleasant ornamental gardens and a good place for a stroll and a picnic. The muddy Yarra is often called 'the river that flows upside down', but there is still plenty of activity along its banks. If you want to join the cyclists, you can hire a bike from under Princes Bridge. You can also take a boat cruise, departing from Princes Walk (just below Princes Bridge) and Southgate. The gardens are also the setting for the Moomba Waterfest, held here over the Labour Day weekend at the beginning of March. Moomba is a celebration of the city and Australia's largest community festival.

Heading past the boatsheds on your left, you'll come to the **Riverslide Skate Park,** where it's fun to watch the skateboarders doing their kick flips, hand plants and other such acrobatics. Across Alexandra Avenue are **Queen Victoria Gardens**, with several interesting modern sculptures as well as the Floral Clock *(see page 53)*.

Above: the entrance to Luna Park
Right: Australian Centre for Contemporary Art

The National Gallery and Victorian Arts Centre

After exploring the gardens, cross St Kilda Road to the **National Gallery of Victoria (NGV) International** (www.ngv.vic.gov.au).

Founded in 1861 as the Museum of Art, this is Australia's oldest public art gallery. After extensive redevelopment and the completion of a second building the collection is now split. The **Ian Potter Centre: NGV Australia** at Federation Square *(see page 45)* is dedicated exclusively to Australian art, while **NGV International** at St Kilda Road (open daily 10am–5pm; tel: 8620 2222) is home to the gallery's impressive international artworks.

The European gallery of the NGV International exhibits paintings, prints, drawings and antiquities, including works by Picasso, Monet and Poussin. It holds the finest collection of paintings by European Old Masters in the southern hemisphere. The celebrated *Banquet of Cleopatra* by Tiepolo and Rembrandt's *Two Old Men* are among the collection.

Before exploring the rest of the arts complex, take a detour to see the **Australian Centre for Contemporary Art** (take tram No. 1 – or walk – down to 111 Sturt Street; open Tues–Sun 11am–6pm; tel: 9697 9999; www.acca online.org.au). Recently opened, a dramatic, rusting edifice rises up in urban homage to the massive steel sculptures of contemporary artist Richard Serra.

Back at the north end of Sturt Street, you can't miss the **Victorian Arts Centre** (www.vicartscentre.com.au), with its 162-metre (530-ft) high spire pointing to the sky. The installation of a complex lighting system on the spire in the 1990s has meant that this cultural icon now has a dramatic night-time presence on the Melbourne skyline.

The Arts Centre, flagship of the performing arts in Melbourne, is comprised of the Theatres building, the Sidney Myer Music Bowl and Hamer Hall. The first, topped by the spire, houses three theatres and is built on an enormous scale; the underground section alone reaches six levels below St Kilda Road, and is serviced by 70 dressing rooms.

The largest of all the centre's venues, the **State Theatre** makes a startling impact. Marble-topped bars, walls of mirrors and red plush interspersed with original Australian artworks set the scene for entry to this auditorium, where musicals, opera, ballet and a range of commercial productions are performed. The **Playhouse Theatre**, renowned for its Aboriginal artworks,

concentrates mainly on drama, as does the **Fairfax Studio**, home of the Melbourne Theatre Company.

Concerts and Tours

Hamer Hall (until recently the Melbourne Concert Hall), is considered one of the world's greatest auditoriums. Its spectacular interior, painted in the

colours and patterns of the country's mineral and gemstone deposits, gives the impression of having been carved out of a hillside. The hall, located next to the Southgate development and Princes Bridge on the Yarra River, was originally designed for symphony orchestras, but has been acoustically tuned to suit a variety of musical styles.

The building houses the **Performing Arts Collection** (www.vicartscentre.com.au/pam/), about 200,000 items relating to the history of theatre in Australia, including costumes (such as Dame Edna Everage's frocks and glasses), set models, props, puppets, photographs, posters, programmes and personal memorabilia. Access to the collection is through the museum's research service.

Other venues coming under the umbrella of the Victorian Arts Centre include Blackbox, for stand-up comedy and modern music, and the Sidney Myer Music Bowl, on the other side of St Kilda Road, through Kings Domain Gardens, which is an outdoor venue *(see page 53)*.

One-hour guided tours of the whole complex (subject to availability, Mon–Sat at noon and 2.30pm; 90-minute backstage tour on Sun at 12.15pm; children under 12 not permitted) give a good overview.

Top: National Gallery of Victoria (NGV) International
Above: ceiling mosaic in NGV International

The Sunday Market (every week, 10am–5pm; tel: 9281 8581), along St Kilda Road between Hamer Hall and Theatres Building, is a great place to look for original gifts and souvenirs; stallholders sell hand-crafted items such as scarves, ceramics and jewellery.

Leaving the arts precinct, walk towards the Yarra River and take any of the connected pathways or stairs down to the Southbank area. The main attraction here is the Southgate development – a shopping and dining complex overlooking the river. At the Riverside Food Court you can sit inside or outside on the terrace and enjoy a meal or a glass of wine while watching the bustle on the river. Try the River Seafood Grill (open 11.30am–late; tel: 9690 4699; www.riverseafoodgrill.com), on the mid level, for fresh fish and river views; or check out the Blue Train Café (tel: 9696 0111; www.blue train.com.au), which opens early for breakfast. Every Sunday between 1 and 3pm free entertainment is laid on (tel: 9699 4311).

But the pleasure of this place is not just in the eating or shopping – a walk along the promenade, with city skyscrapers just across the river, has become as much a part of the Melbourne experience as watching a football match at the MCG *(see page 47)* or sunbathing at St Kilda beach.

4. THE CITY GRID – NORTH OF BOURKE ST *(see map, p22)*

Starting right in the heart of Melbourne's retail mall, this tour bags the best shopping areas and includes a walk through Chinatown. It ends at the new Melbourne Central Shopping Centre.

Catch any city-bound tram or any loop-bound train and get off at Flinders Street or Melbourne Central station. Both are a short walk to the mall

Shopping is a big thing for Melburnians. With a higher standard of living and more disposable income than many Western nations, Australians love to spend. The rejuvenation of many retail districts in Melbourne reflects this consumerism; it also shows a desire by the authorities to lure shoppers back to the city centre, away from the outlying suburban malls.

Begin this tour on the corner of Bourke and Swanston streets. The **Bourke Street Mall**, a short pedestrian and tram-only strip, has some magnificent arcades and small boutiques, and is home to the city's two main department stores, Myer and David Jones (Australia's equivalent to John Lewis). The mall received a makeover in time for the 2006 Commonwealth Games.

The network of arcades and lanes in the city centre is by far the largest and most complex in Australia. When Melbourne's central grid was laid out in 1837, Robert Hoddle, disagreeing with Governor Sir Richard Bourke, insisted on vast streets – 30 metres (99 ft) wide instead of Bourke's favoured 20 metres (66 ft). As a compromise Hoddle gave way to Bourke's enthusiasm for having alternate lanes running east–west. These lanes, many of which retain something of their 19th-century character, were to be

Right: one of the Three Businessmen in Bourke Street

one-third the width of the main streets, and were intended to serve the stables and outer offices of buildings fronting the major streets. Gradually the lanes were transformed into little streets (Little Bourke Street, etc.) and arcades.

Royal Arcade

To the south of Bourke Street Mall is the **Royal Arcade**, the oldest of Melbourne's surviving arcades. The roof features cast-iron scrolls decorated in red and gold. Glass skylights allow natural light to flood into the passageways.

Above the entrance you can see one of the city's better-known landmarks: a magnificent clock which features two elaborately painted 2-metre (7-ft) pine figures, Gog and Magog, which have been striking time on the hour for many years. Modelled on figures erected on the Guildhall in London in 1708, they symbolise the mythical conflict between ancient Britons and Trojan invaders. The arcade has a variety of speciality shops, including some selling antiques and stationery. It's also worthwhile exploring the connecting arcades.

Leaving the arcade and going back onto the mall, you can't miss the extravagant Victorian architecture of Melbourne's former General Post Office, now transformed into a retail development combining shops, a health spa, restaurants and street cafés. Cross Elizabeth Street and continue straight down Bourke Street until you come to Hardware Lane on your right.

As its name suggests Hardware Lane was once lined with warehouses. It's now a pretty pedestrian lane paved with red brick and lined with green bollards and a colourful sea of café umbrellas. There are shops selling camping equipment, some specialising in arts and crafts, and several cafés and bistros, including Campari Italian Restaurant (tel: 9670 3813; www.campari.com.au) – a good spot for lunch, unless you fancy a Chinese meal.

Chinatown

Turn right at Lonsdale Street and right again almost immediately at stone-paved Niagara Lane, which features another picturesque warehouse at Nos 25–31. Turn left at the end of Niagara Lane and walk straight along

Little Bourke Street until you come to Chinatown.

On the east side of this intersection, the entrance is highlighted by an Oriental gateway. This has been the focal point for the Chinese in Melbourne since the days of the gold rush. In the 1850s the Chinese opened their stores here alongside boarding houses, brothels, herbalists and opium dens. Half the fun of a walk through Chinatown is turning down some of the cobbled lanes and finding interesting eating places and attractions. One such place is the **Museum of Chinese Australian History** (open daily 10am–5pm; tel: 9662 2888) at 22 Cohen Place. The long Chinese dragon, Dai Loong, who comes out to celebrate the Chinese New Year, lives on the ground floor.

After exploring the side streets, continue up to the top of Little Bourke Street and turn left at Spring Street then left again at Lonsdale Street. You'll see the **Comedy Theatre** (tel: 9209 9000; www.marrinertheatres.com.au/cn venues.htm) on your left, with an attractive Florentine-style exterior. Opened in 1928, it has been added to the Historic Buildings Register.

Across the junction of Russell Street with Lonsdale Street is the city's newest retail attraction, **QV** (tel: 9658 9658; www.qv.com.au). Taking up a whole city block, this striking example of urban design combines apartments and commercial space with new retail outlets, restaurants and cafés. For exclusive designer fashion try Albert Coates Lane; if you prefer youth and street culture, then check out Red Cape Lane.

Turn right at Swanston Street and walk a block until you come to the **State Library** (open Mon–Thurs 10am–9pm, Fri–Sun 10am–6pm; tel: 8664 7000; www.slv.vic.gov.au), Australia's oldest free public library. The majestic presence of the building stands as a testament to the philanthropism of Melbourne's early leaders, who envisaged a great antipodean state, where all would have access to education and the arts. Take time to soak up the atmosphere and browse through the library's mind-boggling collection of books; you can also get free internet access. Throughout the year, the State Library organises a range of exciting programmes and events, from exhibitions and displays to lectures.

Directly across the road is the **Melbourne Central Shopping Centre** (www.melbournecentral.com.au). Opened in 1991, the centre recently underwent extensive renovations. The ambitious new design, which incorporates a plethora of retail shopping and the Hoyts Cinema complex (previously located on Bourke Street), links up the retail complex to Melbourne Central Railway Station.

Left: inside the Royal Arcade, with Gog and Magog
Above: shopping in Chinatown

5. ACROSS THE BAY AT WILLIAMSTOWN *(see map below)*

A full-day tour beginning with a ferry trip from the city centre, and taking in some of Williamstown's maritime history. The day ends on the beach.

Begin this tour either by taking a ferry from Southgate Pier, situated next to Flinders Street Station, or catch a train to Williamstown.

The coastal village of Williamstown is a popular place for visitors and Melburnians alike. On summer weekends the place is heaving, and with good reason; this early colonial settlement is quite charming, and world's apart from the commercial bustle of the city.

The quickest way to get to Williamstown from central Melbourne is by train (regular departures from Flinders Street Station). However, for a more interesting trip, two ferry companies vie for business from Southgate Pier: Melbourne River Cruises depart from Southgate Landing every hour from 10.45am–3.45pm (www.melbcruises.com.au); or Williamstown ferries leave Southgate pier 7 every half an hour from 10.30am–5pm (tel: 9686 4646; www.williamstownferries.com.au). The hour-long ferry trip winds its way down the Yarra River past the industrial wastelands of Melbourne. While it's by no means a scenic trip it gives you an insight into some of the more undeveloped areas and passes under the monstrous West Gate Bridge. An optional stop on the ferry is the **Scienceworks Museum** at Spotswood (open daily 10am–4.30pm; tel: 9392 4800; www. scienceworks.museum.vic.gov.au). This is the science and technology section

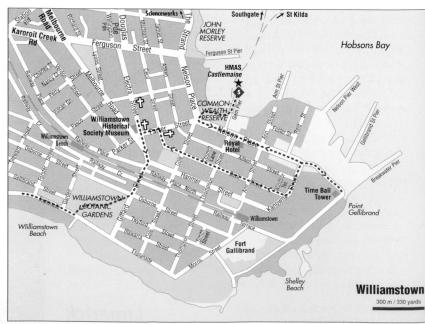

Williamstown

300 m / 330 yards

of the Museum of Victoria, built on the site of Melbourne's first sewage works. Here you can inspect old machines, push buttons and pull levers to find out how things work; children love it. It also incorporates a planetarium (shows on the hour 11am–3pm; www.museum.vic.gov.au/planetarium).

The ferry arrives in Williamstown at **Gem Pier** – a good starting point for a walking tour. Gem Pier was built by convicts in 1839, and replaced in 1847 with a more stable pier that could be used for commercial shipping.

Nelson Place

Nelson Place lies in front of the pier. While it was once a thriving harbour, it did not feature the grand streets and gardens that are here today. During the 1840s passengers had to be carried from their ships on the shoulders of seamen and were dumped onto a muddy shore lined with saltbush. All this changed in the 1850s when the gold rush began and thousands of diggers were drawn to Victoria. Ships crammed into Hobsons Bay and shops, pubs and ship-repair works sprang up along the Nelson Place shoreline. By 1870 Williamstown was known as the major cargo port of Victoria, with piers, slipways, shipwrights and gangs of 'wharfies' working along the shore opposite Nelson Place.

In 1887 engineers finished work on the Coode Canal. By cutting out a long, looping bend in the Yarra, where the river wound through the West Melbourne swamp, the canal brought ships right into the heart of Melbourne, bypassing Williamstown. Gradually Nelson Place and the harbour at Gem Pier became a bit of a backwater in which old buildings could survive. With its 19th-century buildings, its boating activity and surviving boat-building industries, the area is a rich reminder of the grandeur and bustle of Melbourne's first seaport.

HMAS *Castlemaine*, berthed at Gem Pier (open weekends noon–5pm), holds a collection of nautical exhibits and memorabilia from the past. The ship, built in Williamstown, served during World War II in the coastal and northern waters of Australia, the Pacific, the Indian Ocean and the China Sea. If you opted out of the ferry trip to Williamstown you could still get good views of the bay and Melbourne's skyline from the bow of the ship.

Commonwealth Reserve is in front of Gem Pier. Around the reserve are several historic markers and objects moved from elsewhere in Williamstown, including the anchor of a Victorian Navy vessel, the *Nelson*. The *Nelson* was launched in 1814, and was the largest wooden battleship of the Napoleonic Wars era. In 1864 she sailed to Melbourne to become the flagship of the Victorian Navy.

Standing alongside the anchor, the Tide Gauge House is a convict-built structure (like many others in Australia), constructed in 1860. The little

Left: paddling on the beach in Williamstown
Right: street cafés in Williamstown

bluestone building had special automatic machinery which recorded tides at Williamstown up until 1943.

From here walk east along Nelson Place, keeping the sea to your left, past the magnificent buildings in the Nelson Place shopping strip. These were built to serve the rich port trade. Ships' chandlers, sail makers, pubs and shipping offices traded with the world's sailing fleets as they passed through Williamstown. Banks took up the best sites in Nelson Place, many of them built from the massive profits made during the 19th-century gold rushes.

Keep walking straight down Nelson Place past the former **Royal Hotel** at No. 85. All ports had their hotels or pubs (the two can be synonymous in Australia), places for a last drink with friends, a first stop for sailors after months at sea, and a refuge for lonely immigrants on their first night ashore. Now a boarding house, the old Royal remains a local landmark. Its bright red and white facade can be glimpsed by sailors and ferry passengers as they round Point Gellibrand and head for Williamstown or the Melbourne docks.

Continue in the same direction along Nelson Place right to the edge of the shore and you'll come to Point Gellibrand and the Time Ball Tower. You'll pass various cafés and restaurants; Mussels Fish and Chippery is a 1950s-style fish and chip café.

History and Horticulture

Point Gellibrand is one of the most important historical sites in Victoria. The first government-owned railway opened here in 1859 with steam trains running from the piers to Spencer Street. Convicts built the **Time Ball Tower** (1851–52) and the **Breakwater Pier** (1855–60) in bluestone. Its corners set

Above: boats against the city skyline
Left: statue in a Williamstown park

to the points of the compass, the tower has been used for hydrographic surveys and as a lighthouse, but its name originates from the copper ball dropped each day, enabling ships' navigators to set their watches.

Retrace your steps back along Nelson Place as far as Kanowa Street and go left for two blocks, then turn right at Cecil Street. Continue down Cecil Street past one of Melbourne's few two-storey wooden houses until you come to the Mechanics Institute, at 5 Electra Street, which houses the **Williamstown Historical Society Museum** (open Sun only 2–5pm; tel: 9397 5933). The museum collection covers maritime history, furniture, costumes and general exhibits relating to life in Williamstown from the early days of settlement.

From here walk south to **Williamstown Botanic Gardens** (tel: 9932 1114; www.parkweb.vic.gov.au). With winding gravel pathways, colourful flowers and some rare tree specimens dating from the 19th century, the gardens are a perfect spot for a casual stroll or picnic break. They were the first suburban botanic gardens in Melbourne and have retained much of their original layout, with elements from Edwardian and later plantings.

Walk through the gardens down to the Esplanade and past the striking cream-coloured building with a central round tower – the bather pavilion dating from the 1930s. Continue along the Esplanade to the beach. Originally popular with working-class families from the western suburbs, during the inter-war years it also attracted many country visitors who stayed in local boarding houses for a summer holiday by the sea. More recently a shark-proof net has been strung out to protect swimmers at the beach.

6. COLLINGWOOD AND FITZROY *(see pull-out map)*

This tour starts in one of Melbourne's finest gardens, then takes a tram ride to the city's bohemian heart, where you will find street displays, trendy cafés and quirky shops.

To get to Fitzroy Gardens, the start of this tour, from the city catch tram No. 48 or 75 from Flinders Street and hop off at Lansdowne Street

These two inner-city suburbs have managed to maintain some of their working-class roots. High-rise luxury flats are not common here – instead you'll find a great mixture of fine terrace houses from the Victorian era, high-density public housing commission flats, and student housing. The suburbs are a lively mix of artists, students, migrants and trendy inner-city dwellers.

Start the walk in the tranquillity of **Fitzroy Gardens** (www.fitzroygardens.com), just east of the city grid, bounded by Clarendon Street, Albert Street, Lansdowne Street and Wellington Parade. A fine example of 19th-century landscaped gardens, they are beautifully laid out over 26 hectares (64 acres), with historic buildings and sculpture. The first building of interest is **Cooks' Cottage** (open daily 9am–5pm; tel: 9419 4677; www.cookscottage.com.au), originally built in England

Right: Captain Cook's statue at his parents' cottage

in 1755 by the parents of Captain Cook. English navigator James Cook (1728–79) discovered the east coast of Australia; he dropped anchor in Botany Bay in 1770 before sailing north, charting 4,000km (2,500 miles) of coast. Eight years later the first fleet of convicts and soldiers arrived.

The stone cottage, given to the city as a gift at Victoria's centenary celebrations in 1934, was dismantled and transported from the village of Great Ayton to Melbourne, where it was reassembled in its original state. Inside the cottage, the rooms are set out with original or reproduced furniture, in the style of homes in the north of England in the mid-1700s. The doorway has

a stone lintel with the initials of Cook's parents, James and Grace, and the year of construction carved in it. Tours and educational programmes are run from the cottage.

An authentic mid-18th century garden, of the kind that could have existed in North Yorkshire at the time of Cook's childhood, has been created around the cottage, and the surrounding parkland of trees and shrubs were transported here specially from England.

From Tudor to Tropical

The English theme of the garden continues with the model **Tudor Village**, just north of Cooks' Cottage. The London borough of Lambeth offered this representation of a typical English village to Melbourne in gratitude after its residents sent food to Britain during World War II. The village features cottages, a church, a school, a hotel and a scale model of Shakespeare's home and Anne Hathaway's cottage.

Next to the Tudor village is **The Fairies' Tree**, which is carved on the stump of one of the original 300-year-old red gum trees. Carried out between 1931 and 1934 by artist Ola Cohn, the carvings feature likenesses of fairies, dwarves and gnomes, as well as koalas and other Australian animals, and appeal especially to children. "I have carved in a tree in the Fitzroy Gardens," said the artist, "for you and the fairies, but mostly for the fairies and those who believe in them, for they will understand how necessary it is to have a fairy sanctuary."

Continue exploring the gardens and you'll come across the **Conservatory** (open daily 9am–5pm). Built in 1929, it contains an impressive variety of flowering plants, with its displays changed five times a year. Blazing poinsettias contrast with tropical foliage in the winter months, while a vibrant sea of cyclamen and cinerarias heralds the end of winter.

Leave the gardens at the north side on Albert Street, turning left and continuing until you come to Morrison Place, where you turn right. Continue for one block until you reach the tram junction on the Victoria Parade corner.

Above: the Fairies' Tree
Above Right: in Fitzroy Nursery. **Right:** public art, Brunswick Street

Jump on a No.11 tram going down Brunswick Street and get off at the Moor Street corner (or ignore the tram and continue walking for 15 minutes). Here you are entering Fitzroy and Melbourne's funkiest, most alternative shopping and eating areas.

Brunswick Street Experience

Brunswick Street is the area of Melbourne which best reflects the city's soul. Here, people from all walks of life, from those with multiple body-piercings to smartly dressed business people, come to enjoy the vibrant atmosphere and try out one of the numerous unpretentious cafés. The allure of this bohemian, shabby-chic café culture has led to its expansion into the surrounding streets. The best thing is to explore for yourself.

Among the many groovy shops, you'll come across Out of the Closet, selling recycled clothing and Scally and Trombone, specialising in hats and jewellery. Elsewhere you can pick up bondage wear, records, books – try PolyEster Books at No. 330 for underground books, films and comics – and surgical supplies. Some shops tread a fine line between retail outlet, coffee shop ('caffeine dealer') and bar; it's all part of the Brunswick Street experience to wander in and out, stopping for a drink or coffee, browsing and people-watching.

A variety of independent art galleries are to be found around here; in the early 1980s a boom in art-school graduates increased the demand for gallery space, and young artists banded together to establish their own galleries.

There are also numerous public artworks between Moor and Westgarth streets, including pavement mosaics, sculptures, seating with the ceramic mosaic finish which can be found on several works in the city, wacky bicycle stands and Gothic noticeboards. Many of the innovative shop signs were designed and manufactured by local artists and are sculptures in themselves. There appears to be particular rivalry between purveyors of greenery:

the extravagant ornamental gates of the Fitzroy Nursery featuring multi-coloured three-dimensional animals and plants are surpassed only by Vasette, the area's hippest florist, where giant flowers run riot over the walls and roof; one flower sculpture, the size of a lamppost, stands to the side, with a gleam in its eye as it chomps on a bee from the swarm clamped to the building.

The restaurants along this strip reflect Melbourne's multiculturalism. As in the rest of inner Melbourne, you'll find great Thai, Vietnamese, Greek, Italian and Chinese restaurants, but here you'll also encounter Indian, Ethiopian, Afghan and a host of others. The music and bars ensure that the delights are not just culinary ones.

For a quick and tasty snack, try the perennially popular Black Cat Café at 252 Brunswick Street, or for good-value café fare go to The Fitz at No. 347 or Café Provincial on the corner of Johnston Street. Polly Bar at No. 401 is a little cocktail bar with a decadent, 1920s burlesque feel. Also along Johnston Street (between Brunswick and Nicholson streets) is Melbourne's Spanish quarter. Here you'll find a collection of tapas bars and restaurants, many of them featuring live flamenco music.

More Art

After Brunswick Street turn right down Johnston Street and left into George Street. At No. 404 is the **Centre for Contemporary Photography** (open Wed–Sat 11am–6pm, Projection Window daily 6pm–1am; tel: 9417 1549; www.ccp.org.au), with large, purpose-designed galleries.

Return to Johnston Street and continue down until you come to the Wellington Street junction, where you can see a **Keith Haring mural** on the wall of Collingwood Technical School, facing the Tote, one of Melbourne's many live music pubs. This mural was one of two major pieces painted by the controversial American artist in 1984. Although Haring, who died in 1990 aged 31, is now recognised as a world-ranking painter and designer, Melburnians hotly debated the significance of this mural before a project to stabilise the wall and prevent further deterioration was given the go ahead.

7. SOUTH YARRA, PRAHRAN & TOORAK *(see pull-out map)*

A tour that takes in the areas where Melbourne's wealthy live, eat, shop and play. It includes a visit to a marvellous National Trust colonial mansion and one of the best food markets in the city.

Start this tour in the southeast corner of the Royal Botanic Gardens. Take tram No. 8 from Swanston Street in the city

This is a very upmarket part of Melbourne. You will see smart cars, designer shops and fancy restaurants in abundance; when Melburnians want to spend serious money, they head for the shopping streets of South Yarra, Toorak and Prahran (pronounced 'P'ran'). These three adjoining suburbs have now become one distinct area to explore.

From the Royal Botanic Gardens, walk up Dallas Brooks Drive and board Toorak tram No. 8 in Domain Road (or you can get on at Swanston Street). The tram will take you along Toorak Road where you will pass tree-lined streets on which stand palatial homes. This is a must on the itinerary of Japanese and other regional tourists who peer in wonder at the superb old houses and ostentatious new ones set in their vast gardens. It's no surprise that this suburb boasts Melbourne's highest proportion of millionaires. Get off on the corner of Williams Road at stop 34, turn left and walk up the hill until you come to Como House.

Colonial Como

Como House (open Tues–Sun 10am–5pm; closed Good Friday and Christmas Day) is a marvellous National Trust building which started life in 1847 as a single-storey villa. Over the next 30 years the modest villa became a gracious colonial mansion – a consequence of social aspirations and the wealth generated by the gold rush and later pastoral development. The Armytage family lived here from 1864 for 95 years. In 1959 the National Trust acquired Como complete with an extensive collection of original furnishings.

The house is fascinating to wander through and its history is re-told by enthusiastic guides. At the time of the first European settlement in 1835

Left: hotspot in Brunswick Street
Above: interior of Como House

the land overlooking the Yarra River, where the house was later built, was known as the Wurundjeri area, as it was the traditional hunting ground of the Woiworung Aboriginal people. Twelve years later Melbourne had a population of just 10,000 people when the single-storey house was constructed of rendered rubble walls made from mud stone taken from the banks of the Yarra.

The gardens are also a pleasure to explore, with sloping lawns, flower walks, cypress glades and impressive water fountains.

Leaving Como House, turn right into Williams Road, then right again to go back along Toorak Road.

Eating and Entertainment

The shops along Toorak Road and in the arcades off it are exclusive and expensive; you can buy English soaps, perfumes and toiletries, rich chocolates, silk underwear and designer clothes. After a few blocks you will come to the Chapel Street intersection. On one corner stands the **Como Centre**, an upmarket shopping and cinema centre under one of Melbourne's most luxurious hotels, and on the other corner is Freedom Furniture, a homeware store, and Q.bar, a trendy nightclub and celebrity haunt. Head down Chapel Street; where Toorak Road is 'establishment', Chapel Street is bold and brazen. There are still plenty of expensive fashion stores, but nestled in among these is a smattering of shops with unusual clothes at cheaper prices, appealing to a younger, funkier crowd.

On the left-hand side you will come to the **Jam Factory** – once, amazingly enough, a jam factory, but now a glitzy shopping complex enhanced by the ancient boilers, stained glass and colourful pipes. Largely American in style, it contains a multiplex cinema, fashion stores and scores of bars and restaurants.

If you need sustenance at this point, try the Ay Oriental Tea House at No. 455 Chapel Street – it offers yum cha, tea and even tea-based alcoholic drinks (open daily 10am till late) – the Kazbar at No. 481 for a coffee, or The Greek Deli and Taverna at Nos 583–85 for lunch or dinner. With Melbourne having the largest Greek population outside Greece, the national dishes are a speciality.

Continue along Chapel Street and turn right down Commercial Road. The grand old building on the left-hand corner is **Pran Central**, another upmarket shopping centre, this one converted from the original Prahran Station, still complete with copper domes, art-nouveau stained glass and decorative ironwork giving it a bright and appealing feel.

On the right-hand side of Commercial Road is **Prahran Market** (open Tues dawn–5pm, Thurs and Fri dawn–6pm, Sat dawn–5pm, Sun 10am–3pm),

Above: Chapel Street scene

a must-visit site for all foodies and market-lovers, especially on Saturday mornings when the place is humming with colour and noise and delicious smells. Buy some freshly baked bread, olives and cheese and enjoy an ad hoc lunch, supplemented by free tastings, or take a snack in one of the surrounding cafés. On Sundays you'll find live jazz and children's activities.

The other attraction of Commercial Road is the great selection of bars, restaurant and cafés, although this time with a twist – most of the businesses along this stretch are gay-owned.

Retrace your steps once more up to Chapel Street and walk the three blocks down to Greville Street. On this corner stands the **Prahran Town Hall**, built in 1861 in Victorian Italianate style; today it is used as a venue for stand-up comedy, as well as fashion shows and exhibitions. This area, once a haven for hippies, has become seriously trendy in recent years. It is at its finest on Sundays between noon and 5pm, when **Greville Street Market** in Grattan Gardens springs to life. The stallholders sell a wide variety of items, from arts and crafts, jewellery and vintage clothes to delicious freshly made food.

8. THE NORTH SIDE OF THE YARRA *(see map, p46)*

This tour starts at Federation Square, then moves along the banks of the Yarra to the Melbourne and Olympic Parks.

Start the tour at Federation Square, opposite Flinders Street Station.

Federation Square (tel: 9658 9658; www.federationsquare.com.au) is the new cultural heart of Melbourne, completed in 2002. This ambitious project, built over the city's main railways lines, brings together shopping, arts, parks, sports and entertainment in a striking architectural complex, paved in colourful stone from Western Australia's Kimberly region. With a capacity of 15,000 and large-screen videos, this is a great place to watch sporting events.

At the corner of Swanston and Flinders streets is the Melbourne Visitor Centre (open daily 9am–6pm; tel: 9658 9658), a convenient first stop to discover what's going on in the city. But the biggest attraction is the **Ian Potter Centre: NGV Australia** (open Mon–Thurs 10am–5pm, Fri 10am–9pm, Sat–Sun 10am–6pm; tel: 8662 1553; www.ngv.vic.gov.au), the first major gallery dedicated exclusively to Australian art, featuring a suite of galleries covering Aboriginal art.

Also in the square – across four levels of the Alfred Deakin building – is the **ACMI** (Australian Centre for the Moving Image; open Mon–Fri 10am–5pm, Sat and Sun 10am–6pm; tel: 8663 2200; www.acmi. net.au), a state-of-the-art facility illustrating the development of the moving image from

Right: Melbourne Visitor Centre

early cinema to the latest digital technology. And for horse-lovers, there's the Australian Racing Museum, called **Champions** (tel: 1 300 139 407).

East of the square is **Birrarung Marr Park** – the first area of parkland to be created in the city for over 100 years. The 8.3-hectare (20-acre) park features a children's theatre, a café and cycle paths, but most intriguing of all are the **Federation Bells**. These are a set of computer-controlled bells which play specially commissioned pieces on a daily basis.

A Passion for Sport

Continue walking along the river and you can't miss the **Melbourne and Olympic Parks** on your left. Together they comprise a number of world-class structures hosting a wide range of sporting and entertainment events. The **Rod Laver Arena** is home to the Australian Open Tennis Championships, the first of the year's Grand Slam tournaments. If you want to get a taste of what it's like to play on a world-class court you can book one (tel: 9286 1244).

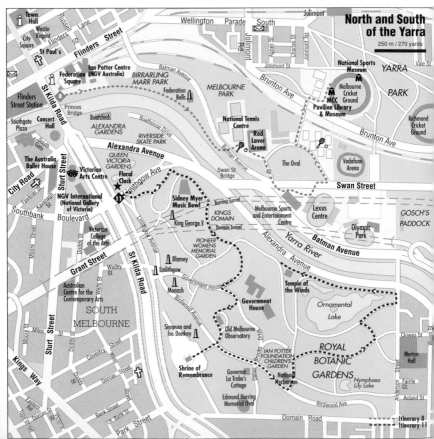

Nearby is the **Vodafone Arena**, completed in 2000, with a retractable roof. The 10,000-seat multi-sports and entertainment venue includes a velodrome (cycle-racing track), basketball and tennis courts (key Grand Slam tennis matches are played here as well as at the Rod Laver Arena); it is also used for concerts and conferences. The Oval next door is another huge venue.

Across Swan Street, renovations have been completed at the last remaining building from the 1956 Melbourne Olympic Games, the **Lexus Centre**. Now home to AFL club Collingwood Magpies, it incorporates an elite sports complex while also serving as an events and function centre (www.lexuscentre. com.au). The **Olympic Park Stadium** to the north has a soccer pitch, an athletics track and concert facilities.

When the Game isn't Cricket

North of the Vodafone Arena, over a footbridge crossing the tram and train lines and Brunton Avenue, is **Melbourne Cricket Ground** (MCG; tel: 9657 8861; www.mcg.org.au), home to Test Series cricket matches and Australia's most popular sport, Australian Rules Football. Australia's first football match was played in 1858 by cricketers looking for an off-season sport. The game thrived on the rivalry and class differences between the suburbs and the fierce pride of the players and fans. The game has changed but the passion remains. Saturday afternoon watching football continues to be an intrinsic part of life for thousands of Melburnians and, more recently, for fans all over Australia. The MCG underwent major redevelopment ahead of the Commonwealth Games and now has a capacity of 100,000 and facilities on a par with the world's best.

The cricket ground is one of the biggest stadiums in the world and has been graced by countless sporting heroes, celebrities and world leaders, from the Pope and Queen Elizabeth II, to Australia's most famous cricketer, Donald Bradman. One-hour guided tours depart from the Great Southern Stand regularly, between 10am and 3pm, except on event days. The Australian Gallery of Sport and Olympic Museum will find a new home in the National Sports Museum (scheduled for completion in November 2007), located in the huge space that is **MCG City**. This is the museum and entertainment precinct of the redevelopment and will also house the Sport Australia Hall of Fame, the Australian Cricket Hall of Fame and the Aussie Rules Exhibition.

The MCC (Melbourne Cricket Club; www.mcc. org.au) library and museum is scheduled to reopen in November 2006, next door to the Australian Gallery of Sport and Olympic Museum.

If you want to extend this tour and feel like something different, head for Richmond, known as Little Vietnam. Catch a tram or walk down Swan Street as far as Church Street, then take tram No. 78 or 79 north to Victoria Street. Here you'll find a huge range of terrific but inexpensive Vietnamese restaurants, as well as grocers selling anything from Kung Fu shoes to smoked duck.

Left: rowing up the river
Right: high emotion in Australian Rules football

9. ALBERT PARK *(see pull-out map)*

The serenity of the lakes and parks more than makes up for aching feet on this long walk. Just don't attempt to do it in early March – most of the route is also the site of the Australian Grand Prix.

Start this tour at the north end of Albert Park. Tram No. 12 from Collins Street or No. 1 from Swanston Street will take you there.

Much of the pleasure of exploring Melbourne is discovering its parks and gardens, and one of the best is **Albert Park**. Established in the 1860s the 225-ha (556-acre) park features an artificial lake surrounded by parkland. The lake was once a lagoon teeming with wild fowl and a place of great importance to local Aborigines. After it was cleared and fenced much of the park was given over to cattle grazing.

At first called South Park, it was renamed following the death of Queen Victoria's consort, Prince Albert, in 1861. At that time St Kilda Road formed the eastern boundary. During the 1970s work was begun to transform the shallow lagoon into a lake suitable for boating. Boathouses were built, yacht and rowing clubs established and a promenade formed around the lake edge.

For many people, simply strolling around or taking a picnic to eat by the lake is the best way to enjoy the park. The 11 picnic areas have free electric barbecues, playgrounds and shelters. You can also observe some of the park's waterbirds from the wetlands. But bird-watching and walking are two of the more sedate activities in the park. The Albert Park Yacht Club and Sailing Club, in Aquatic Drive, conducts races on the lake every Saturday. Boats and aquabikes are also available for hire by casual sailors, rowers and canoeists.

Behind the sailing clubs is the Bob Jane Stadium, home to the South Melbourne Football Club, and beyond that, in the northwest corner of the park, is the **Melbourne Sports and Aquatic Centre** (open Mon–Fri 5.30am–11pm, Sat, Sun and public holidays 7am–8pm; tel: 9926 1555; www.msac.com.au).

Above: sailing on Albert Park lake

It is the largest leisure and sporting complex in Australia, with a wide range of recreational facilities. For fun in and around water, there's a wave pool, water slide, spas, a sauna and steam room, as well as swimming pools. As with the Melbourne Cricket Ground, the complex recently underwent renovations for the 2006 Commonwealth Games.

Golf and Aughtie Drive

Next to the Aquatic Centre is the **Albert Park Golf Driving Range** (golf bookings tel: 9510 5588; driving range tel: 9696 4653; www.golfvictoria. com.au/range), with a 270-metre (890-ft) range, 60 tee positions, fairways, a putting green, pitching area and sand bunkers. Remind yourself that you are going to finish the walk, and continue on round the lake – the trail around the circumference of the lake is 8 km (5 miles). From the path you can see much of the park's wildlife: many species of birds, possums and, beneath the water's surface, turtles and a profusion of tiny silver and golden perch.

Continue walking around the park between Aughtie Drive and the lake. **Aughtie Drive** is part of the Formula One Grand Prix circuit, Australia's biggest annual sporting event. Held in early March the staging of the event has not been without controversy. Locals and park users have protested over the effect the race, with its noise and crowds, would have on wildlife and the surrounding areas. But many of their voices were silenced when house prices rose and economic benefits were seen.

Along this section of the lake are a couple of kiosks and a restaurant, The Point, which are handy if you haven't packed a picnic. From the viewing tower attached to The Point restaurant you can see the 18-hole golf course across the lake and skyscrapers in the city.

The walk finishes at an historically interesting site, of great Aboriginal significance. Evidence suggests that the Aborigines inhabited Albert Park and its surrounds 40,000 years ago, when the area was a wetland with sand dunes around salt lagoons. The **Corroboree Tree**, in the southeastern corner of the park, is the 40-metre (132-ft) high river red gum tree, reputed to be the meeting place for members of a coastal tribe, and now the only remaining link with the early inhabitants. Historical accounts record white settlers watching

Aboriginal corroborees – as the gatherings were called – in the Albert Park area in the early days of white settlement. These tribes shaped and managed the land through periodic harvesting and hunting. The Corroboree Tree stands surrounded by a busy highway on one side and a quiet swamp with native plants on the other. It is believed to be between 300 and 700 years old. Though much has changed, the recent plantings and the swamp nearby give some idea – if only a rather vague one – of what this area was like before European settlement.

Left: Formula One racing in Melbourne

10. CARLTON *(see map, p51)*

Just north of the city centre, Carlton is home to the World Heritage listed Royal Exhibition Building and the new Melbourne Museum. In contrast you can also explore Little Italy.

Melbourne City Baths are an easy walk from the city centre. Alternatively you can catch any tram going north on Swanston Street.

Start your tour at the grand old **Melbourne City Baths** (open Mon–Thurs 6am–10pm, Fri 6am–8.30pm, Sat and Sun 8am–6pm, public holidays 10am–6pm; Closed Good Friday, Christmas Day, Boxing Day, New Years Day; tel: 96635888; www.melbournecitybaths.com.au), which stand on the corner of Swanston and Victoria streets. The baths were opened in 1860 following a Yarra River typhoid scare, and Melburnians flocked to enjoy the luxury of a bath. A report in the 1950s found the baths to be in a 'disgusting state of neglect' and they were closed down in the 1970s. Saved from demolition and restored, the baths today feature swimming pools, a gymnasium, squash courts and a spa and sauna. The original atmosphere of the building, however, is still there, with potted palms, tiled floors, stained-glass windows and the old slipper baths.

Prison with a Past

Walk east along Victoria Street until you come to the **Old Melbourne Gaol** (open daily 9.30am–4.30pm; closed Christmas Day and Good Friday; tel: 9663 7228), near the corner of Russell Street. While only one cell block remains, the gaol is worth a visit for the stark images of 19th-century prison life. Here prisoners were incarcerated not only from the outside world, but from their fellow inmates, and a strict rule of silence was enforced. At the time of construction, in 1845, however, it was considered to be very advanced.

One hundred and thirty-five prisoners were hanged here, including the infamous Ned Kelly, who was a kind of 19th-century Robin Hood. His death mask, and those of other prisoners, are on display.

Although much of the fabric of the prison has vanished, its appearance has been reconstructed with help from old documents – maps, drawings, photographs and written descriptions.

Victorian Style

On leaving the gaol rejoin Victoria Street and turn left down Rathdowne Street where you will find **Carlton Gardens**, home of the magnificent Royal Exhibition Building, and the new Melbourne Museum, opened in 2000.

Specially constructed for the Melbourne International Exhibition of 1880, the

Left: Old Melbourne Gaol. **Right:** Melbourne Museum reflecting Royal Exhibition Building

Royal Exhibition Building (tel: 9270 5000; www.museum.vic.gov.au/reb) is the first building in Australia to be granted World Heritage status. When it was built, Melbourne was a prosperous city, basking in riches brought from the gold rush, and the optimism and energy of the age is reflected in the grand style and soaring dome of the exhibition pavilion. For many years it was the largest building in Australia, attracting spectacular events like the Centennial International Exhibition of 1888 and the opening of Federal Parliament in 1901. It has taken everything in its stride – housing the Victorian State Parliament, an influenza hospital, an art gallery and museum, an air-force depot, a migration centre, a war memorial and a number of government offices. The opulent interior has now been meticulously restored, and you can take a guided tour (tel: 1300 130 152; start at Melbourne Museum).

Just north of the Royal Exhibition Building is the **Melbourne Museum** (open daily 10am–5pm; closed Good Friday and Christmas Day; tel: 8341 7777; www.melbourne.museum.vic.gov.au), a new high-tech multimedia museum which aims – through 'exploration, education and fun' – to give visitors an insight into Australia's flora, fauna, culture and way of life. There are innovative exhibitions on Aboriginal culture and a living rainforest with native animals. The interactive children's museum will keep the little ones happy, while the huge **IMAX theatre** *(see page 75)* is ideal for older children.

Leave the gardens at the north end, walk along Grattan Street and turn right at **Lygon Street**. This is the home of Melbourne's café culture, started when large numbers of Italians settled here in the 1950s, hence the nickname **Little Italy**. The Victorian terraces are crammed with cafés and restaurants serving delicious pizza, pasta and *gelati*. For good-value pizza try Papa Gino's at No. 221. Il Gambero next door serves similar fare and is a favourite with students, while you can

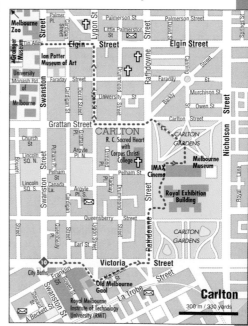

get good coffee at Café Trevi opposite. Further down Lygon Street you'll find bookshops, galleries and trendy clothes shops. The crowd here is mixed, with students from the nearby university joining the literary set stocking up at the bookshop Readings. Further along, in the Lygon Plaza, you'll find the Cinema Nova, a large arthouse complex showing a variety of old and new films. The best time to visit this area is October for the Lygon Street Festa, a celebration of Italian culture and one of Australia's largest outdoor street festivals.

University of Melbourne

Turn left at Elgin Street and straight ahead is the **University of Melbourne** (www.unimelb.edu.au). There are a number of Gothic-style buildings nestled among the brick blocks, and during term times there are often bands playing, markets in full swing, or other activities going on in the open grounds.

There are also many museums and galleries within the university. One of the better ones is the **Ian Potter Museum of Art** (open Mon–Fri 10am–5pm; tel: 8344 5148), which displays 19th- and 20th-century Australian art, early glass, antiquities and ethnographic material, and was renovated in 2004. (It should not be confused with the Ian Potter Centre: NGV Australia in Federation Square.) The **Grainger Museum** (closed to the public until 2005; tel: 8344 4000) was established in the 1930s by the composer and pianist Percy Grainger to show 'the sources from which composers draw their inspirations.' The rather eccentric collection includes displays of music, musical instruments, furniture, costumes, ethnographic materials and collections relating to other Australian composers. Also within the grounds is the **Medical History Museum** (open Mon–Fri 8.30am–10pm, Sat 11am–5pm), which documents the history of medical practice in Victoria, and includes a fully equipped relocated 19th-century London pharmacy, as well as medical and scientific instruments and early medicine chests.

You can extend this tour if you're feeling energetic; **Melbourne Zoo** (open daily 9am–5pm; tel: 9285 9300; www.zoo.org.au) is about one kilometre (half a mile) to the northwest of the university (from the city centre, take tram No. 55 from William Street Mon–Sat, or tram No. 68 from Elizabeth Street on Sun). Opened in 1862, it is the oldest zoo in Australia and the third oldest in the world. The zoo displays a sample of the world's fauna and flora in different bioclimatic (habitat) zones, including such native delights as the southern hairy-nosed wombat and the Victorian koala bear.

Above Top: dining alfresco in Lygon Street
Above: Melbourne University shield

11. THE SOUTH SIDE OF THE YARRA *(see map, p46)*

A stroll through Melbourne's best-loved gardens – the Royal Botanic Gardens – including a visit to the Old Melbourne Observatory and the Shrine of Remembrance.

The starting point is the Floral Clock in Queen Victoria Gardens. Any tram going south along Swanston Street will take you there.

This tour explores the large area of parkland on the south side of the Yarra known as the King's Domain, which includes what many say are the finest gardens in Australia, the Royal Botanic Gardens. If you want to explore by bike, you can hire one from under Prince's Bridge in **Alexandra Gardens** *(see page 30)* and cycle by the river's edge along the Yarra River Trail.

In **Queen Victoria Gardens**, near the junction of St Kilda Road with Linlithgow Avenue, is the Floral Clock, presented to the city by a group of Swiss watchmakers in 1966. Across Linlithgow Avenue in Kings Domain you'll see the **Sidney Myer Music Bowl**. Built in 1959 but newly renovated, this outdoor music and entertainment venue is a Melbourne icon. Heading down the park, past the Pioneer Women's Memorial Garden, stands Government House, built between 1872 and 1876 at the height of Melbourne's boom years. Modelled on Queen Victoria's Osborne House on the Isle of Wight, this grand stately home is rarely open to the public. When the white flag is flying from the landmark white square tower, you know the governor is home.

Adjacent to Government House is the **Old Melbourne Observatory** (open Fri–Mon 10am–4pm; presentations Tues 7.30–9pm; tel: 9252 2429), dating from 1861. Although long since stripped of its astronomical function, the observatory is open for tours.

The Shrine of Remembrance

Leaving the observatory, cross Birdwood Avenue to head towards the imposing **Shrine of Remembrance** (open daily 10am–5pm except Christmas Day and Good Friday; www.shrine.org.au). A significant Melbourne landmark, the shrine was built in 1934 as a tribute from the people of Victoria to mark the sacrifices made in World War I. The forecourt with its eternal flame and cenotaph was added to recognise service in World War II, while the Remembrance Garden commemorates later conflicts in Korea, Vietnam, Malaya, Borneo and Kuwait, and peace-keeping operations in Afghanistan and Iraq. The man and donkey statue in the west forecourt represents Simpson, a soldier who rescued wounded men at Gallipoli by carrying them away from the front line on his donkey. A subterranean visitor centre was opened in August 2003, providing improved access for the elderly and disabled, and better educational and exhibition facilities.

The central point of the sanctuary is the **Stone of Remembrance**. At 11am on

Right: Simpson and his donkey at the Shrine of Remembrance

the 11 November, the time when hostilities ceased in World War I, a ray of light shines through an aperture in the roof and rests on the word 'Love'.

The Botanic Gardens

If you leave the observatory and cross Dallas Brooks Drive you will come to the **Royal Botanic Gardens** (open Apr–Oct daily 7.30am–5.30pm, Nov–Mar daily 7.30am–8.30pm; tel: 9252 2300; www.rbg.vic.gov.au), one of the great gardens of the world. Established in 1846 by Charles La Trobe, the design we see today – sweeping lawns, meandering paths, rocky outcrops, attractive vistas and an ornamental lake at its centre – was created in the late 19th century by the then director, William Guilfoyle.

The gardens contain a vast range of plants from all over the world, and are an ideal sanctuary for many native birds and animals. The plants are all beautifully laid out in their respective climatic zones. You can see rainforest giants (on the Australian Rainforest Walk), desert cacti, alpine wildflowers and temperate shrubs in a landscaped setting. No one knew how well trees and plants from other parts of the world would grow in Melbourne when planting began in cleared bushland in 1846. But the four English elms put in then are still in place. On one of the highest parts of the gardens is the **Temple of the Winds**, built by Guilfoyle as a tribute to Charles La Trobe, the founder of the gardens; standing on this 19th century folly, you can see sweeping views of Melbourne.

Near the junction of Birdwood Avenue and Dallas Brooks Drive is the **National Herbarium of Victoria**, which has more than a million plant specimens used for plant classification, identification and conservation. Between the herbarium and the observatory is the recently opened **Ian Potter Foundation Children's Garden** (open Wed–Sun 10am–4pm, closed Christmas Day, Boxing Day, New Year's Day and Good Friday; closed for maintenance 11 July 2005–6 September 2005), an interactive hands-on experience for children of all ages. Here the aim is for kids to learn about nature while having fun; they can pick flowers, get their hands dirty, scramble around in overgrown plant tunnels and find out what's croaking in the pond.

Near Observatory Gate is a café, and there's a tearoom and kiosk beside the ornamental lake for meals or snacks.

12. FLAGSTAFF, QUEEN VICTORIA MARKET AND NORTH MELBOURNE *(see map, p56)*

Visit Melbourne's most famous market and wander through the streets of north Melbourne with its railways, wharves, goods sheds and market buildings.

The starting point is Flagstaff Gardens. The free city circle tram from Spring, Flinders, La Trobe or Spencer streets will take you there.

Inner north and west Melbourne has traditionally been linked with the transport, storage and sale of rural produce from other parts of Victoria: wool from the Western District, wheat from the Wimmera and Mallee, cattle from most parts of the state. In the early 1880s the area had the highest population density in the city. The residents were mainly working class and about half were Irish Catholics.

Begin the tour in **Flagstaff Gardens**, the site of some of Melbourne's earliest historic sites: old burial grounds, an observatory which served as the magnetic survey of the colony, and a flagstaff commemorating the time when the hill was the centre of the town's communication system.

In 1840 a tall flagstaff was erected here, on what was then the city's only vacant hill in sight of port shipping. Its signal flag announced the first sight-

ing of a vessel, its anchoring, or any mishap such as it running aground. Perhaps the most important news for the Port Phillip settlement came from the hill in 1850 when Victoria was proclaimed a separate colony from New South Wales. Four years later the advent of the electric telegraph made the flagstaff obsolete.

Nearby, a memorial erected in 1870 marks the grave sites of some of the town's pioneers; dating back to 1836. In the 1860s the park was fenced and planting began along the serpentine pathways which linked the park's six gates. In the 1880s fashions changed and many pines and gums from the original planting were replaced by the shade trees (elms and oaks) which survive today.

Visiting the Market

Leaving the gardens, walk north up Peel Street to **Queen Victoria Market** (513 Elizabeth Street, tel: 9320 5822; www.qvm.com.au; open Tues–Thur 6am–2pm, Fri 6am–6pm, Sat 6am–3pm, Sun 9am–4pm). Dating from 1878, this is the biggest and most central market, and even runs to an information office where organised tours can be booked (the Foodies Tour departs every Tuesday, Thursday, Friday and Saturday at 10am, while the Heritage Market Tour explores the market's history; tel for both tours: 9320 5835).

Left: the Royal Botanic Gardens
Right: *tai chi* in Flagstaff Gardens

There's a huge array of fresh produce – the fruit and vegetables alone are spread over four sheds – as well as speciality stalls stocking obscure delicacies from all over the world (unless they have to be imported and fall foul of the stringent customs regulations – you won't find foie gras here for example). The Deli Hall, built in 1927, retains many of its original art deco features such as marble counters, the equivalent of today's refrigerated cabinets. If it's cold or wet, take refuge in the heated Food Court, which offers take-aways and seating for about 400; the food ranges from fish and chips to Southeast Asian.

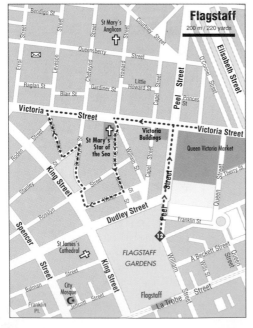

A huge area is devoted to clothing, footwear, leather, linen, sports gear and tourist souvenirs. On Sundays the whole place becomes a vast general goods market and buskers swarm in to make the most of the crowds. Queen Street is closed and becomes an outdoor café area, with children's rides and other activities taking place.

In the summer months a night market operates (Dec–Feb, Wed 5.30–10pm), where the focus is on food and entertainment; the new age section offers tarot readings and bizarre gifts.

city itineraries

Meander Through North Melbourne

Leave the market on Victoria Street, turn left and you'll come to the **Victoria Buildings**, opposite the Victoria Hotel. Queen Victoria's subjects were devoted, if unimaginative. The Victoria Buildings predate the market structures by 14 years and, like many 19th-century commercial rows, are made up of three shops pretending to be one. Just down the street you can see the old Royal Exchange Hotel, one of many sleek art deco buildings to be found in the area.

The Don Camillo Coffee Lounge at No. 215 Victoria Street is a good place to stop for a breather. The inner suburbs have absorbed many ethnic groups, and during the 1950s and 60s the cluster of shopkeepers along this part of Victoria Street was mainly Italian. Until recently Don Camillo housed the first coffee machine in post-war Victoria – a gleaming chrome number – but it's now to be found in the Melbourne Museum *(see page 51)*. However, with its terrazzo floor and 1950s wire furniture, the café still sums up an era. Up-stairs is the restaurant, while an empty bandstand recalls headier days.

Now cross William Street to view **St Mary's Star of the Sea Catholic Church** (open daily 8am–6pm). Built in a French Gothic-Revival style, the church's unfinished state reflects the waning of the area's population as the rapidly expanding city's warehouses and factories replaced housing. Walk down the aisle to the altar and admire the vaulting above the choir. On the way out, look at the rich decoration of the organ pipes in the loft above.

A few metres down William Street follow Howard Street to the right. On the corner with Rosslyn Street is another gloriously restored art deco build-ing. Across the road Howard becomes Milton Street, which holds more row-house architecture, wedged in among factories of the 1920s and 30s, as well as later development connected with the publishing industry. Turn right at Walsh Street and right again at King Street where you will see the Victorian Labor Party HQ.

To the right, across Rosslyn Street, follow Chetwynd Street, turn left at Stanley Street and head up Eades Place. Here you will find a school which helped set the pattern for government schools until the 1920s. Although orig-inally designed in the 1840s to take 1,100 children, about 2,300 children's names were on the roll when it opened. Less than half that number attended, the rest being left to the mercy of the truant of-ficer. A century later, enrolments had sunk to little more than 40 – an indication of the degree to which housing had been replaced by warehouses and factories.

Go left at Victoria Street, and you'll come to the Coles prefabricated house at No. 456. Few buildings have survived from the 1850s when these streets were laid out, but this one is an exception. It reflects the colony's rapid growth during the gold-rush era when both tradespeople and building materials were in short supply.

You can catch a tram from Victoria Street back into the city centre.

Above Left: Queen Victoria Market
Right: pastoral image

13. Docklands and South Melbourne *(see map, p59)*

Here we explore the new Docklands area, visit an historic sailing ship and take a stroll through South Melbourne to the popular South Melbourne Market.

Take the free City Circle tram to the corner of LaTrobe Street and Harbour Esplanade.

To the east of the city, beyond the Telstra Dome, is Melbourne's Docklands area, a vibrant precinct in the midst of development. You can take the 048 NewQuay Docklands tram direct from Flinders Street to Dockland Drive and the Harbour Esplanade, or a ferry (weekends only; tel: 9682 9555). Walk along to NewQuay, the waterfront community overlooking the harbour, lined with cafés

and restaurants, and watch the activity in the marina. Boat tours will take you around the harbour (Tram Boats, tel: 9379 0406; Pleasure Boats, tel: 9620 5620), or to view Melbourne's fairy penguin colony, on a rock structure built in Port Phillip Bay for the 1956 Olympic Games (Penguin Waters, tel: 9386 8488; www.penguinwaters.com.au).

Walk back past the Telstra Dome, where sports matches are held, and head south to the river through Docklands Park. On the way you'll see a good deal of striking urban art, including Reed Vessel, a stainless steel streamlined construction raised up in the park. Cross the Yarra via Webb Bridge, then head east along South Wharf.

Maritime Heritage

You'll come to the **Melbourne Maritime Museum** (open daily except Good Friday and Christmas Day, 10am–4pm; tel: 9699 9760). The central exhibit of the museum is the *Polly Woodside*, a beautifully restored 19th-century sailing ship, moored in the original wooden dry dock (the only one of its kind remaining in the world). Built in Belfast in 1885, the ship rounded the infamous Cape Horn 16 times, carrying coal and nitrate between Europe and South America. Sold to the National Trust in 1968 in a very bad way, she was restored by volunteers. Today visitors can walk the deck of the tall ship, admire the complexity of the rigging, and see the cramped conditions in which the crew lived. Other exhibits in the museum include maritime artefacts, shipwright tools and photographs explaining the development of the dock, river and surrounding area since the 1950s.

Exhibition Centre and a Mega Casino

Just past the museum is the **Melbourne Exhibition Centre**, which stages national and international coventions and exhibitions. Former State Premier Jeff Kennet was the force behind this and many of the city's other striking new developments *(see page 16)*. It is informally known as 'Jeff's shed' by the typically wry Melburnians.

Above: Melbourne Exhibition Centre aka Jeff's Shed
Right: the Crown Resort Casino by night

On the other side of Clarendon Street, dominating the River Yarra, is the huge **Crown Entertainment Complex**. This centre features a five-star hotel, the largest casino outside North America, Australia's biggest ballroom, many restaurants, brasseries, bistros and bars, cinemas, a theatre and designer shops. Much of the appeal of the centre is simply strolling through it, watching the glamorous high rollers, window shopping, or having a drink at one of the bars. You can also watch and listen to the **Four Seasons sound and light show** in the five-storey marble atrium.

South Melbourne Market

When you've had your fill of glitz, head into the streets of South Melbourne. You can either walk down Clarendon Street, or take tram Nos. 12, 96 or 108, until you come to **South Melbourne Market** (open Wed 8am–4pm, Fri 8am–6pm, Sat and Sun 8am–4pm) on the corner of Cecil and Coventry streets. Established in 1867, this covered market is one of the most popular in the city, with a wide range of stalls selling clothing, quirky handicrafts and interesting gifts, as well as all kinds of delicious things to eat. Food/cooking tours are available (tel: 9209 6295 for information and bookings), and street musicians playing jazz, blues and Cajun music add to the festive atmosphere.

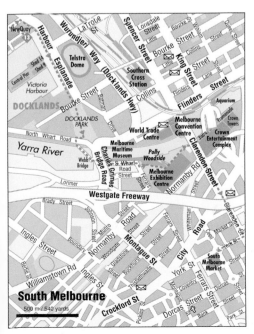

Excursions

Excursion 1. Dandenongs and Yarra Valley *(see map, p62)*

A day-long exploratory tour east of the city into the bush of the
Dandenong Ranges and the lush Yarra Valley. This tour, which includes
visits to wineries, must be done by car. You could extend it by staying
overnight in a Yarra Valley B&B.

The **Dandenong Ranges**, only about an hour's drive east of the city, make
for a delightful break from city life. A favourite escape for Melburnians
since the boom times of the 1880s, they are dominated by soaring mountain ash forests and lush tree-fern gullies.

Take the Eastern Freeway and Maroondah Highway which leads to **Lilydale**, or take the South Eastern Freeway and Burwood Highway which goes
to **Upper Ferntree Gully**. Both are at the foot of the Dandenongs and make
ideal points to begin your exploration. Along the forest tracks you'll see
the world's tallest flowering tree, the mountain ash, which creates the high
shady canopies. The sunnier, drier northern and western faces of the range
feature woodlands of box and stringybark. The birdlife, dominated by laugh-
ing kookaburras, crimson rosellas (parrots) and cockatoos, helps provide the
soundtrack. Most of the range's native animals – the owls, possums, bats and
gliders – are nocturnal, but in daylight hours you could easily come across
an echidna or wombat scratching at the forest floor.

The villages in the ranges are as charming as their names suggest: Kallista,
Clematis, Olinda, Sassafras and Ferny Creek, to name a few. The first white settlers, who came to log wood and mine gold from around 1870, and later to escape the dirt of the city, constructed beautiful weatherboard guesthouses with
enormous verandahs, fine churches and quaint village shops.

Especially popular with children is the **Puffing Billy steam train** (runs
daily except Christmas Day; tel: 9754 6800; www.puffingbilly.com.au), which
whistles its way from Belgrave to Gembrook carrying passengers in open car-
riages and closed restaurant cars as it chuffs
through hills and untouched bush, crossing a
creek on a huge wooden trestle bridge.

Cheese and Wine

The rolling green hills of the **Yarra Valley**
are home to around 30 wineries, many of
which offer tours, great food and magnificent
views. Start the tour at Lilydale, which sits at
the beginning of the valley, and en route to
Yarra Glen you'll pass rows of ripening
grapes, and many opportunities to enjoy not
only the wines, but also the numerous local

Left: Puffing Billy
Right: cute koala

cheeses and fruits of the area. The **Yarra Valley Dairy** (McMeikans Road, Yering; tel: 03 9739 0023) is one such place; an old dairy building has been converted into a restaurant where prize-winning hand-made cheeses and local wines are served. The dairy was originally part of the old Yering Station, the first winery you'll come to down the Melba Highway. Established in 1838 as the first vineyard in Victoria, Yering Station now offers great wine and food and cutting-edge architecture.

Surrounding Dixon's Creek you'll find more award-winning wineries, including the **De Bortoli Winery** (Pinnacle Lane; tel: 5965 2271), an excellent place to stop for a wine tasting and panoramic views. Another good winery in the area is **Shantell Vineyard** (1974 Melba Highway; tel: 5965 2155). The 16-hectare (40-acre) property, only developed since 1980, now produces prize-winning wines.

For something different, take a detour to **Healesville Sanctuary** (tel: 5957 2800; www.zoo.org.au; open daily 9am–5pm). More than 200 species of Australian birds, mammals and reptiles live in a bushland setting. As well as koalas, kangaroos and cockatoos, you can visit World of the Platypus.

Excursion 2. Geelong and the Great Ocean Road
(see pull-out map)

Geelong is Victoria's second-largest city, about an hour from Melbourne. The coastline leading west from it is one of the most beautiful coastal stretches in the world. This is an excursion that is best done by car, but there are frequent trains and coaches to Geelong.

To get to Geelong take the Princes Highway out of Melbourne. Leave via the West Gate Bridge where you'll experience great views of Melbourne. Alternatively V/Line runs frequent trains to Geelong from the city's Southern Cross Station (formerly Spencer Street Station; now transformed into a retail-and-office complex and one of Melbourne's most iconic pieces of modern architecture thanks to its unusual rippled roof). V/Line Coaches also operate between Melbourne and Geelong and from main towns along the Great Ocean Road.

While the joy of this trip is the Great Ocean Road, the city of **Geelong** – the name derives from Jillong, the Aboriginal word for the bay – is enjoying a revival and has several attractions worth seeing.

Sheep, Submarines and Surfers

Geelong's Eastern Beach, a short walk from the city centre, is a hive of activity. A great deal of money has been invested in the waterfront, and its landscaped new look is complemented by shops, restaurants, cafés and bars overlooking Corio Bay.

The city's links with the sea are showcased at the **Naval and Maritime Museum** (open daily 10am–4pm; tel: 5277 3808) at Swinburn Street, North Geelong. This site was once home to Australia's submarine fleet. The **National Wool Museum** (open daily 9.30am–5pm; closed Christmas Day and Good Friday; tel: 5227 0701) is located at the corner of Moorabool and Brougham streets. Housed in an 1872 bluestone wool store, the museum documents the history of sheep farming and the wool industry in Australia. Geelong also has numerous fine National Trust properties and historic country gardens.

Before heading for the Great Ocean Road, take a detour via the Bellarine Highway to **Queenscliff**, at the entrance to Port Phillip Bay. Here you can join a boat tour taking passengers out to swim with wild dolphins and seals in the bay (Sea-All Dolphin Swims; Sept–April 8am and 1pm; tel: 5258 3889; www.dolphinswims.com.au). Or, if you prefer not to get wet, you can take a trip on the car ferry that operates between Sorrento and Queenscliff as dolphins often hitch a ride on the bow wave.

Back in Geelong, leave via Torquay Road, which becomes the Surf Coast Highway and then joins the Great Ocean Road. Keep driving south until you hit **Torquay** (Visitor Information Centre open daily 9am–5pm; tel: 5261 4219) – widely considered Australia's surfing capital. The proliferation of surf shops and wave enthusiasts hanging around tell the story. Torquay is a pretty town – wander along its main street and choose a beachfront café for lunch. Alternatively, you could

Above Left: ballooning over the Yarra Valley
Right: surfer at Bells Beach

visit the world's largest surfing museum, **Surfworld Museum** (open Mon–Fri 9am–5pm, Sat, Sun and public holidays 10am–4pm; tel: 5261 4606). Jan Juc and world-famous Bells Beach, home of the Surf Classic at Easter, are located to the south of Torquay. Fisherman's Beach, less prone to big waves, is popular with families, not just fishermen.

An alternative way of exploring the coast is to take a flight in a tiger moth plane. **Tiger Moth World** (daily 10am–5pm, except Tues in winter; tel: 5261 5100; www.tigermothworld.com) at Blackgate Road, Torquay, organises flights all along the coast in its open cockpit World War II vintage bi-planes. For an adrenaline rush you can add aerobatics to the flight, or take a tandem skydive (this is Victoria's biggest skydiving centre). The site also features an adventure park with mini golf, a museum, and picnic areas.

Further along the coast Anglesea is well known for its sheer cliffs. If you fancy a round of golf at the **Anglesea Golf Club** (open daily 11am–sunset), be careful you don't hit one of the many kangaroos grazing nonchalantly on the course. Continuing on from Anglesea, you can't miss Split Point lighthouse at Aireys Inlet, a beacon to Great Ocean Road travellers and a great look-out point. While the tower is not open, the coastal views from the lighthouse reserve are stunning.

Lorne and Erskine Falls

Lorne is the most popular town along this stretch of the coast; set between the sparkling waters of Loutit Bay and the forests of the Otway Ranges, it has special charm and is worth exploring. Lorne's beach is perfect for families, with gentle waves lapping a wide stretch of golden sand.

From Lorne you can also enjoy great bush walks in the nearby **Anga-hook-Lorne State Park**. For a dramatic waterfall, turn right at Erskine Falls Road, just before you come into Lorne proper, and follow the signs to **Erskine Falls**; they are an easy 20-minute hike through the bush. The most popular of the falls cascades 30 metres (98ft) into a beautiful tree-fern gully.

It is when you leave Lorne that you reach the really stunning section of the Great Ocean Road, with sheer cliffs and majestic ocean views on one side and the Otway Ranges and Angahook-Lorne State Park on the other. Many streams and rivers flow over waterfalls on their course to the sea. Pick one of the many marked walking tracks that start from the various picnic areas.

Native Animals and Twelve Apostles

Further along the coast is the Otway National Park, and within the park, about 45 minutes from Apollo Bay, is the spectacular **Otway Fly Tree Top Walk** (open 9am–4pm; tel: 5235 9200; www.otwayfly.com). This is a 600-metre (2,000-ft) steel walkway perched 25 metres (80 ft) high in the rainforest tree tops, providing a walk within the canopy of myrtle beech forest. The thrill seeker can climb to the viewing platform at a height of 45 metres (150 ft).

In the park itself, you're almost certain to see swamp wallabies, which are widespread throughout the ranges. Other species are harder to spot, such as the koala, platypus, bushtail and ringtail possum, bandicoot, eastern grey kangaroo, bats and various species of marsupial mice. About 200 species of birds have been noted, ranging from wrens to the giant albatross. Parrots and cockatoos are common, and you may also spot hawks and eagles.

Cape Otway adjoins the national park, and the light station (open daily 9am–5pm; tel: 5237 9240; www.light station.com) is its focal point. It was only the second lighthouse on the mainland to be constructed, and has Australia's oldest group of lighthouse keepers' cottages.

Near Lavers Hill is the **Melba Gully State Park**, a small pocket of natural rainforest created to protect the area from the ravages of bushfires, which have burnt much of the ranges. But perhaps the most spectacular stretch of the coast runs from Princetown to Peterborough, known as the **Port Campbell National Park**. This is home to the world-famous **Twelve Apostles** (www.12apostlesnatpark.org), giant rock stacks left isolated from the mainland by the erosive power of the ocean. A new visitor centre tells you about the geology and history of the area, and a tunnel under the Great Ocean Road leads to the viewing platforms. The park also offers much evidence of earlier Aboriginal life here.

Above Left: Split Point lighthouse. **Left:** the Twelve Apostles
Right: natural rainforest in Melba Gully State Park

Leisure
Activities

SHOPPING

If you like shopping, you'll love Melbourne. Whether you're into off-beat grunge fashion or the latest in designer numbers, the city will provide what you need. With great markets, spanking new shopping centres, bargain-basement retailers and trendy streets and arcades, the difficulty will be not spending too much.

Opening Hours

Some shopping precincts have unrestricted shopping hours, but most stores open Mon–Thurs 9am–6pm, Fri 9am–9pm and Sat 9am–5pm. Sunday shopping is commonplace, too, with major city department stores and shopping centres open 9am–4pm. Many pharmacies are open 12 hours a day, seven days a week, and a lot of convenience stores, supermarkets and fast-food restaurants stay open 24 hours a day.

Australiana

There are speciality stores in most shopping precincts selling all kinds of 'Australiana' products aimed at tourists. These include the usual array of Akubra hats, Drizabone coats, toy kangaroos, fluffy koalas and other species of Australian wildlife, as well as other souvenirs. A good proportion of the goods in these stores are overpriced and tacky. A better bet is to buy gifts from markets, where you can find unusual products and, on occasion, good-quality arts and crafts.

Some of the itineraries already featured in this guide take you on walks past shopping precincts and markets. The best of these, and others that have not already been featured, are listed in this section, with details of their particular specialities. Have fun roaming around looking for your kind of gift or souvenir.

City Centre

All the big department stores are in the city centre. Myer has been a Melbourne institution since Sidney Myer opened his department store in the Bourke Street Mall in 1911. During the depression of the 1930s he took a cut in profits rather than sack staff.

The company, now owned by a leading store investor and the Myer family, is Australia's biggest retailer and takes 20 cents of every dollar spent in the country. The store spreads over three buildings and its vast frontage in the Bourke Street Mall has spawned the saying 'they've got more front than Myer,' to describe someone who has a great deal of confidence.

Also in the mall is David Jones, a slightly more upmarket version of Myer. In and around the mall are numerous shopping arcades and lanes. The area bounded by Swanston, Elizabeth, Bourke and Flinders streets contains a maze of arcades connecting with smaller city streets and lanes. Many of the latter retain something of their 19th-century character. A number of the smaller streets have been renovated and building facades restored.

One such arcade is the Block Arcade *(see page 24)*, near the corner of Collins and Elizabeth streets, which has a fine cathedral-like dome and classic Victorian

Left: sculpture on the Southbank
Right: tacky souvenirs

(see page 24)

architecture. It is home to purveyors of elegant leather, glass and haute couture, and a number of cafés.

Running off Block Arcade is Block Court, on the left going towards Elizabeth Street, an impressive art-deco retail arcade built in the late 1920s. It is housed in what used to be the old Atheneum Club, where gentlemen used to be able to stay, conveniently close to their business pursuits. Note the distinctive 'jelly-mould' plaster ceilings and mosaic flooring. Just to the north, Royal Arcade is another elegant place to shop, with a number of specialist stores such as stationers and antiques shops.

On the other side of Bourke Street, the former GPO building has been converted into a smart new shopping centre; while further along Elizabeth Street is one of the biggest retail complexes in Australia, Melbourne Central, now renovated to house around 300 stores.

Another huge shopping centre is QV on Lonsdale Street *(see page 35)*. An old favourite worth visiting is the Australia on Collins shopping centre, on Collins Street. The Parliament end of the street, known as the Paris end, features exclusive designer ware, including Bally, Hermès, MaxMara, Ferraud, Cartier and Ferragamo. Collins Place shopping centre also at this end of the street, has a name for stylish local designers.

The Southgate Shopping Centre and shopping complex at Crown Casino or Southbank are both 1990s building developments. Crown is the place for upmarket shopping, catering to the high rollers and lucky winners. Southgate has a good mix of speciality and chain stores.

Finally the city centre is also home to Melbourne's biggest and most popular market, Queen Victoria Market (open Tues and Thur 6am–2pm, Fri 6am–6pm, Sat 6am–3pm, Sun – general goods only – 9am–4pm). The market's site is a reminder of the role of north and west Melbourne as an outlet for rural produce. A cattle market traded at the corner of Elizabeth and Victoria streets in 1842 but in 1859 the site was reserved as a wholesale vegetable market. Today, in addition to fruit and vegetables, there are sections for meat, fish, bakery goods, delicatessen items and general merchandise including clothing, shoes, gifts, toys and homeware. From late November to late February a 'Gaslight market' is held (open Wed 5.30–10.30pm), where you can enjoy world food and world music while buying hand-made crafts.

Above: interior of Melbourne Central shopping centre

Toorak Road, Chapel Street and Greville Street

These streets take in the affluent suburbs of Toorak, Prahran and South Yarra *(see page 43)*, and the shops reflect this. Toorak Road is cosmopolitan and slightly establishment. More grand and glamorous than cheap and cheerful, many of the stores feature international designer fashions. Como Centre, an upmarket shopping and cinema centre, is on the corner of Toorak Road and Chapel Street. Toorak Village shopping centre is a 15-minute walk east from here, also on Toorak Road.

Chapel Street becomes a bit funkier and cheaper. The stores here concentrate on up-to-the-minute fashions by local designers. In addition to the usual array of chain stores selling music, books, clothing and homeware, there are two shopping centres in the street, Pran Central and the Jam Factory, a glitzy American-style complex complete with shops, restaurants and cinemas. Prahran Market (closed Mon and Wed, *see page 44*), a good spot for lunch, runs just off Chapel Street on Commercial Road.

Greville Street becomes even funkier still. It's a great place to shop for night-clubbing gear, retro clothing and chic jewellery. The street holds a market on Sunday from about noon.

Brunswick Street

Brunswick Street, Fitzroy *(see page 41)*, is the best of the bohemian – similar in style and feel to Prahran's Greville Street but on a bigger scale. Here you'll find funky clothing, retro stores, bric-a-brac, and some small art galleries.

St Kilda

One of Australia's oldest and longest-running arts and crafts markets is held here on the Upper Esplanade every Sunday. Most of the goods on sale are made by the stallholders themselves. The market throbs with life and is the ideal place to buy an unusual gift. Acland Street is one of Melbourne's most popular food precincts, best known for its speciality cake shops. The delicatessens have a distinctly Eastern European flavour.

Bridge Road and Swan Street

Richmond is the centre for fashion bargains. These two streets specialise in factory outlets, seconds stores and charity shops. As it's a Greek and Vietnamese-inhabited area, there is also a good mix of ethnic bars and restaurants.

Lygon Street

Lygon Street *(see page 51)* is the place to go for a taste of Europe. Italian designer stores are nestled in among Mediterranean-style cafés and restaurants. The top end of the precinct has a shopping centre, Lygon Court, with cafés and cinemas as well as shops.

Docklands

For shopping on the waterfront, try the new Docklands development *(see page 58)* to the west of the city.

Suburbs

Many of the outer suburbs also have vast shopping centres, which usually feature all manner of shops, cafés, bars and restaurants. The best of these are the Chadstone Shopping Centre in Chadstone and Highpoint Shopping Centre in Maribyrnong in west Melbourne.

ight: selling clothes in Prahran

EATING OUT

Melbourne is the undisputed food capital of Australia. It has also long been recognised by top chefs as one of the food capitals of the world. It's hard to eat badly here. With an abundance of fresh ingredients, the world's best seafood and a great mix of different cultural cooking styles, you won't go hungry.

With access to some 3,000 restaurants, embracing more than 70 different varieties of international cuisine, Melburnians are fortunate in the wide selection of exotic food. Eating out is a part of daily life, whether it's an Italian *gelato*, a bulging *schwarma* or a gourmet dinner in a five-star restaurant. No matter where you go in this city, or what hour of the day or night, you will stumble across fabulous cafés, bars and bistros.

Melbourne has entire streets devoted to restaurants, cafés and bars. Lygon Street in Carlton is a little piece of Italy, offering delicious pasta, pizza and *gelati*; Chinatown, in Little Bourke Street, specialises in sticky buns, *yum cha* and Peking duck; while Swan Street, Richmond, offers a great variety of Greek tavernas serving pita, Greek dips, *souvlaki* and chargrilled seafood. Victoria Street in Abbotsford is Little Saigon, with a staggering array of Vietnamese restaurants serving hundreds of dishes at bargain prices. For the flavours of Spain, try Johnston Street in Fitzroy which has door-to-door tapas bars and restaurants. Along Sydney Road in Brunswick you can smell the aromas and spices of Turkey.

Otherwise Brunswick Street in Fitzroy, Acland Street and Fitzroy Street in St Kilda, Chapel Street and Toorak Road in South Yarra all have multiple grazing stops along their strips.

One of the best ways to experience Melbourne and enjoy a meal at the same time is to ride the world's only tramcar restaurant, a colonial dining car which gives visitors and locals an enjoyable perspective of Melbourne's leafy boulevards and best attractions. The **Colonial Tramcar Restaurant** (tel: 9696-4000; www.tramrestaurant.com.au), feeding visitors since 1983, is the oldest tram in the city. It dates back to 1927 and is elegantly refurbished in Pullman style, with a tone reminiscent of the Orient Express.

The decor features plush burgundy velvet and teak bench seats, with gold etched mirrors, scalloped drapes and brass lamps with tasselled vintage shades. It travels various routes through Melbourne's city and suburban streets. To ensure a smooth ride, stabilisers have been fitted so that not even a glass trembles as the tram glides along. It also has one-way glass windows so diners can enjoy the passing scene without curious gazes to distract them.

The tour lasts between two and three hours; prices vary according to the time of day and season; lunch is around $70 a head and in the evening diners can expect to pay $110 per head.

Below is a brief indication of the wonderful selection on offer in Melbourne. The first is a list of speciality food stores, which can be worth visiting to pick up some food for a lunchtime picnic or evening barbecue. A listing of restaurants follows, with each grouped into one of three price categories based on the cost of a three-course meal for one, excluding drinks and tip.

Left: pavement dining in St Kilda

Markets
Queen Victoria Market
513 Elizabeth Street, City
Tel: 9320 5822; www.qvm.com.au
This is the biggest and most central market; there's a huge array of fresh produce as well as speciality stalls stocking obscure produce like warrigal greens and bunya bunya nuts *(see also page 55)*.

Prahran Market
163–185 Commercial Road, South Yarra
Tel: 8290 1333
Concentrating on fruit, veg, meat, fish and dairy, Prahran Market caters to the well-heeled looking for the finest cuts of meat as well as to the student looking to eke out a tight budget. There's a food court too *(see page 44)*.

South Melbourne Market
Corner of Cecil and York streets,
South Melbourne
Tel: 9209 6925
A little more rough and ready than Prahran Market, and slightly cheaper too. This one also sells kitchenware, clothing, good stationery, etc. *(see page 59)*.

Speciality food and wine stores
Cloudwine Cellars
317 Clarendon Street, South Melbourne
Tel: 9699 6700
Australia's number one retailer of wine from small Australian producers. Wines of high quality yet not widely available.

David Jones Food Court
Lower Ground Floor, Bourke Street Mall
310 Bourke Street
Tel: 9643 2222; www.davidjones.com.au
The magnificent food hall of this long-established department store features select fruits and vegetables, exotic cooking ingredients, fresh meats, fish, cheeses and breads, as well as prepared foods.

Enoteca Sileno
920 Lygon Street, North Carlton
Tel: 9388 8554

Family-run since 1982, this is Melbourne's mecca for superb Italian food and wine. Now relocated to larger premises, you can eat in too; try the porcini and asparagus risotto, or some of the delicious seafood antipasti.

Richmond Hill Café and Larder
48–50 Bridge Road, Richmond
Tel: 9421-2808; www.rhcl.com.au
Housed in a Victorian building dating from 1860, this is a well-established shop and café. The food is simple and well-prepared and the cheeses on sale will take your breath away. Also oils, vinegars, bread, pasta and chocolates.

The Vital Ingredient
206 Clarendon Street, South Melbourne
Tel: 9696 3511
Shop alongside Melbourne's chefs and take your pick from the extensive range of local and imported products in this warehouse, filled from floor to ceiling with cooking equipment, condiments and more.

Wild About You Bush Foods
133 Gardenvale Road, Gardenvale
Tel: 9530 6844
Witchetty-grub shaped chocolates, wattle-seed truffles, eucalyptus-leaf mustard and other goodies.

Above: sign for the popular South Melbourne Market

Key to Prices
Inexpensive – up to A$40
Moderate – over A$40 under A$65
Expensive – over A$65
(The dialling code for Melbourne is 03.)

Restaurants

Becco
11–25 Crossley Street, City
Tel: 9663 3000; www.becco.com.au
Becco is found down a lane deep in the city and, with its subdued lighting and discreet atmosphere, is reminiscent of a comfortable club (in the old sense of the word). It offers exquisite Italian-based cuisine and a terrific wine list, all served impeccably. One of the reliable greats in Melbourne dining. Expensive.

Botanical
169 Domain Road, South Yarra
Tel: 9820 7888
Situated on the edge of the Botanic Gardens, this bright modern venue has risen swiftly to become a favourite of the well-heeled habitués of this district of town. The wine list was recently judged Melbourne's finest and the sommelier will find just the right 'sticky' (sweet wine) to accompany the marvellous desserts. Expensive.

Circa, the Prince
2B Acland Street, St Kilda
Tel: 9536 1122; www.theprince.com.au
Consistently hitting the spot, Circa offers a chic dining room for the bon viveurs of St Kilda and beyond. It is renowned for its wine list and knock-out cooking that leans towards Europe. Dress up for that special occasion, or keep it simple and slip downstairs later to see who's playing in the Prince Bandroom. Expensive.

Donovans
40 Jacka Boulevard, St Kilda
Tel: 9534 8221
A St Kilda favourite, Donovans is like an expansive beach house that just happens to serve some of the best food in Melbourne. Service is informal but immaculate, pretty much like the dishes, and you can kick back and relish that holiday atmosphere. Expensive

The Graham
97 Graham Street, Port Melbourne
Tel: 9676 2566
This is a delightful restaurant in a converted pub, where the menu is compact yet ambitious. It's a little off the main tourist routes but more than repays those who make the effort to seek it out. Moderate.

Above: Acland Street in St Kilda is famous for its cakes

Italy 1
27 George Parade, City
Tel: 9654 4430
Tucked away in George Parade, a lane off Collins Street, lies a tiny hidden treasure. Italy 1 serves some of Melbourne's finest Italian cuisine in casually elegant surroundings. Sophisticated and incurably romantic, this seductive restaurant is equally suited to a relaxed get-together with friends or an intimate dinner for two. Inexpensive.

Livebait
55B NewQuay Promenade, Docklands
Tel: 9642 1500; www.livebait.com.au
A seafood restaurant, unrelated to the UK chain, with a strong Mediterranean inclination. The food is very good, although the prime reason for coming here is probably the view across the city and right round to the Bolte Bridge through the great curved wall of glass that wraps around the whole place. Expensive.

mecca
MR3 Midlevel, Southgate, Southbank
Tel: 9682 2999; www.mecca.net.au
Top-notch fusion cooking with particular emphasis on Middle Eastern flavours and ingredients. A very popular restaurant, with great views over the city. Moderate.

Shakahari
201–3 Faraday Street, Carlton
Tel: 9347 3848
This place has been going for years and is still packing them in. First-time visitors to these unprepossessing premises soon discover why. The chef's innovative takes on vegetarian cooking win over the most sceptical carnivores. Inexpensive.

Taxi
Level 1, Transport Hotel
Federation Square
Tel: 9654 8808
After a rather shaky start, Taxi has now established itself as one of the city's finest restaurants. Gaze down at the crowds wandering through Federation Square as you enjoy the work of one of the city's premier cooks along with that of the sushi chef, for the predominant influence here is Japanese. Moderate.

Tho-Tho
66 Victoria Street, Richmond
Tel: 9428 5900
One of a plethora of Vietnamese restaurants in this strip, Tho-Tho is jollier than most with its sea of stylish multicoloured seats, clean lines and prominent bar. It works as a family meeting place or student canteen and the food comes strongly recommended. Inexpensive.

Topolino's
87 Fitzroy Street, St Kilda
Tel: 9534 4856
Pizza and everything else Italian are served until late at night in this dingy St Kilda standby where nobody can see how much the worse for wear you really are. Inexpensive.

Verge
1 Flinders Lane, City
Tel: 9639 9500
This is a prime site in Spring Street to watch the politicians and civil servants come out to play, or, as dusk settles, glimpse the possums frolicking in Fitzroy Gardens. Inside, the adventurous modern cooking is matched by great wines. Moderate.

Waiters Restaurant
20 Meyers Place, City
Tel: 9650 1508
The Waiters' less than glamorous setting down one of the duller alleyways no doubt keeps the overheads down and allows the management to concentrate on providing great food at prices that shame some of the plusher eateries in the area. Inexpensive.

Right: Lygon Street hospitality

NIGHTLIFE

As night falls in Melbourne many of its residents are only just coming out to play. This is when the city really comes into its own, with high-quality theatre, a thriving live-music scene attracting the best new bands, great comedy acts and pubs on every corner. New bars appear down seedy dead-ends and cobbled backstreets, and half the fun is in discovering them for yourself. With fairly relaxed licensing laws, you can usually find somewhere to go drinking 24 hours a day. The downside of this is that if you go early you may be the only punter there. Many bars don't fill up until after 10pm.

The hottest bars and clubs come and go with alarming regularity, so for the latest scene you should check out local publications once in town; try the Entertainment Guide, which comes free every Friday in *The Age* newspaper, and free music publications, such as *Beat* and *Impress*, found in pubs and cafés.

Theatres
Her Majesty's Theatre
219 Exhibition Street
Tel: 8643 3300
www.hermajestystheatre.com.au
Built in 1886 and threatened with demolition in the 1980s, Her Majesty's has now been beautifully restored. Ballet, opera and musical theatre are all performed here.

Malthouse Theatre
113 Sturt Street, South Melbourne
Tel: 9685 5100; www.playbox.com.au
Dedicated to the creation, interpretation and promotion of Australian theatre. The company has gained a reputation for dynamic and progressive drama that reflects Australia's traditions and diversity.

Princess Theatre
163 Spring Street
Tel: 9299 9800
www.marrinertheatres.com.au
This theatre, with its ornate facade, is used for big production musicals.

Regent Theatre and Plaza Ballroom
191 Collins Street
Tel: 9299 9500
The fully refurbished Regent Theatre and Plaza Ballroom was reopened in 1997 to become a new home for theatre and cinema. The Plaza has been recreated as a versatile ballroom and function centre.

Victorian Arts Centre
100 St Kilda Road
Tel: 9281 8000; www.vicartscentre.com.au
Home to Melbourne's performing arts and topped by an enormous spire, the centre *(see page 31)* hosts regular seasons by Opera Australia, the Melbourne Symphony, the Melbourne Theatre Company and the Australian Ballet.

Above: inside the Regent Theatre

Theatre and Event Bookings

Discount Tickets (HalfTix)

Located in the Town Hall (entrance off Swanston Street), this booth sells discount theatre tickets on the day of the performance (except Saturday, when they sell for Sunday shows too). You have to go along in person as there is no phone service. *www.halftixmelbourne.com*

Ticketek

For theatre, sports and event bookings in the city. Tel: 132-849; *www.ticketek.com*

Ticketmaster7

Tickets for all kinds of things can be purchased by phoning 13-61 00 (general events) or 1300 136 166 (theatres); *www.ticketmaster7.com*

Cinemas

Hoyts Cinema Centre

Corner of Swanston and Latrobe Streets
Melbourne Central Shopping Centre
Tel: 8662 3555
www.hoyts.ninemsn.com.au

Greater Union Russell Cinemas

131 Russell Street
Tel: 9654 8133
www.greaterunion.com.au

Village Centre

206 Bourke Street
Tel: 9667 6565
www.villagecinemas.com.au

Kino Dendy Cinemas

45 Collins Street
Tel: 9650 2100
www.dendy.com.au

ACMI Cinemas

Federation Square, Flinders Street
Tel: 8663 2583
www.acmi.net.au

Village Crown

Crown Entertainment Complex
Tel: 9278 6666
www.villagecinemas.com.au

IMAX Theatre

Rathdowne Street, Carlton
Tel: 9663 5454
www.imax.com.au

Bars

Adelphi Hotel Bar

Level 10, 187 Flinders Lane
Tel: 9650 7555

This chic 10th-floor bar offers views across the city. It is hard to find, but worth the effort. It's officially open only to Adelphi Club Members or hotel guests, but a bit of schmoozing in the right department may get you special entry to that place in the sky. The design is all angles, with a narrow swimming pool with a glass bottom jutting out over the street – providing entertainment for pedestrians below. Treat yourself to a cocktail as you gaze over St Paul's Cathedral, down past Flinders Street Station, to Southbank.

Fidel's Cigar Bar

Crown Entertainment Complex
Whiteman Street, Southbank
Tel: 9292 6885

This seductive venue lures you in with its luxurious leather couches and ottomans, cool martinis and a fantastic selection of cigars. Its staff are immaculate and the service very smooth. Fidel's is a great spot for a special nightcap.

Gin Palace

Russell Place, off Little Collins Street
Tel: 9654 0533

Located in the heart of the city, this is the quintessential bar for bohemian elegance. Reminiscent of an old-style theatrical club, it conjures up scenes from a James Bond movie with its superb furniture, ambience, background music and patrons.

The Hairy Canary

212 Little Collins Street
Tel: 9654 2471

Right: mime at Rippon Lea

A Melburnian favourite, since it combines the late hours of a cocktail bar with a groovy café and restaurant that offers substantial fare: antipasti, seafood and pizzas.

The Melbourne Supper Club
1st Floor, 161 Spring Street
Tel: 9654 6300
At the Paris end of Spring Street, the European-styled Melbourne Supper Club cocoons you as soon as you climb the stairs, with its soft ambient lighting, comfy furniture and fabulous antiques. Opposite Parliament House and next door to the Princess Theatre, it's ideally placed for pre- or post-theatre drinks.

Meyers Place
20 Meyers Place (off Bourke Street, between Spring and Exhibition streets)
Tel: 9650 8609
This shoebox bar started the spread of bars in lanes all over Melbourne. Eclectic decor, with shagpile pieces stuck on the wall, quirky offcuts of wood panelling and snug little booths. Meyers Place packs in the crowds and will probably continue to do so. It has survived the fickleness of Melbourne's bar crowd – quite a feat.

Syracuse Restaurant Bar
23 Bank Place
Tel: 9670 1777
In the city's financial business precinct, Syracuse has a striking ambience with high ceilings and an odd assortment of furniture, which includes shelves and cabinets stacked with old souvenir bottles, wine boxes, crates and other ephemera. Features an extensive wine list and interesting menu.

The Purple Emerald
191 Flinders Lane
Tel: 9650 7753
Behind St Paul's Cathedral, this bar is one of several in Melbourne's lanes that have sprung open their renovated doors to reveal a groovy, retro-style interior. Live jazz four nights a week Wednesday to Saturday.

The Kitten Club
2/267 Little Collins Street
Tel: 9650 2448; www.kittenclub.com.au
Perched above the shops with long windows out to the street, the Kitten Club acts as a swish bar with a New York feel, as well as hosting Galaxy Space and the Love Lounge for those who want a bit of turntable action with their drinks. There are regular comedy nights as well.

Misty
Hosier Lane (off Flinders Lane)
Tel: 9663 9202
Tucked away in a lane running alongside the Forum Theatre, this hip place has lots of white curves, with dramatic blocks of colour. A bit grubby round the edges, but still packing in the crowds. Well worth a vodka or too. Light snacks are served as well.

Rue Bebelons Bar
267 Little Lonsdale Street
Tel: 9663 1700
Casual and intimate, with deep-red surrounds. The DJs-cum-bar staff are a multi-skilled crew.

Bars in St Kilda
Mink
2B Acland Street
Tel: 9537 1322
This vodka bar is carved out of the basement of the very cool Prince of Wales Hotel. The spirit of *Pravda* lives on with 43 vodkas, neo-Stalinist comrade art and lots of caviar. However the *pièces de resistance* are the lush, private booths with a switch that manipulates an exterior light. If the light shows green, staff may enter. If it's red, forget it.

The Melbourne Wine Room
125 Fitzroy Street
Tel: 9525 5599
This old corner pub has been transformed into a comfortable wine bar and bistro with a relaxing atmosphere. A great showcase of wines and excellent food.

Above: a sign of Melbourne's best
Right: Melbourne is well known for its nightlife

Dogs Bar
54 Acland Street
Tel: 9525 3599
Located on the ground floor of one of St Kilda's most exclusive apartment blocks, the Dogs Bar is a lively venue with plenty of atmosphere. There is a strong wine list plus impressive platters of antipasti, great pasta and delectable desserts. This is a neighbourhood favourite.

Live Music Venues
Corner Hotel
57 Swan Street, Richmond
Tel: 9427 7300
www.cornerhotel.com
The city's best live music venue, according to many. With a grungy feel and bands playing almost every night, the Corner is a popular venue for a loud night out.

Ding Dong Lounge
18 Market Lane
Tel: 9662 1020
www.dingdonglounge.com.au
With the emphasis firmly on good old-fashioned rock 'n' roll, this place is usually heaving with people after a change from all the electronic lounge bars in the city. Live bands, including big names, appear on a special stage.

Hi-Fi Bar
125 Swanston Street
Tel: 9654 9617; www.thehifi.com.au
A former cinema and grand ballroom, the Hi-Fi now resounds to the noise and vibrations of the latest rock and pop. A great place to catch your favourite band live.

Clubs
Ffour
Level 2, Hub Arcade 318–322
Little Collins Street
Tel: 9650 4494; www.ffour.com.au
With its futuristic lighting (think *Blade-runner*) this bar and nightclub oozes cool.

The Lounge
243 Swanston Street
Tel: 9663 2916
With everything from jungle to funk, this lounge is always open. A happy, laid-back café by day and a happening club by night.

The Metro
20 Bourke Street, City
Tel: 9663 4288
www.metronightclub.com
Big is beautiful at Melbourne's biggest nightclub. The type of music here changes frequently so telephone ahead for the current schedule.

CALENDAR OF EVENTS

Victoria is, undoubtedly, Australia's premier state for festivals and events, enjoying a rich and diverse cultural and sporting life. Throughout the year, there is a rich line up of sporting action, food and wine festivals, and major cultural celebrations – although things are a little thin on the ground around winter and at Christmas time. Note that in recent years, however, many of Melbourne's festivals have been obliged to cease due to spiralling insurance costs. There is no guarantee that a festival that takes place one year will take place the next.

Specific dates for many of the following events vary from year to year. **Tourism Victoria** will be able to give you exact dates (tel: 132 842; www.visitvictoria.com.au; www.visitmelbourne.com).

January

The Australian Open (www.ausopen.org/): Grand Slam partner to the French Open, Wimbledon and the US Open, running for two weeks each January in Melbourne Park. *Midsumma Gay and Lesbian Festival* (www.midsumma.org.au): Melbourne's premier gay and lesbian arts and cultural organisation celebrates the summer.

Australia Day Celebrations (www.australia day.gov.au): a public holiday and an excuse for a huge party, with spectacular firework displays at the end of the day.

February

Melbourne International Music Festival: the country's largest contemporary music festival, at the Sidney Myer Music Bowl.

March

Moomba Waterfest: Moomba means 'having fun,' the aim of this community water festival. The festivities are based around the Yarra River, with colourful street processions, laser displays, waterskiing and fireworks all ensuring that things go with a bang. *Rip Curl Pro*: the world's top-ranked surfers flock to Victoria's surf coast over Easter to compete in the famous Bells Beach classic *(see page 64)*.
Australian Grand Prix: the opening round of the Formula One World Championship. Held around Albert Park Lake *(see page 48)*. *Melbourne Food & Wine Festival* (www. melbfoodwinefest.com.au): showcases Melbourne as the culinary capital of Australia and as one of the world's great cities for dining out.

bove: ladies and hats at the Melbourne Cup

Brunswick Music Festival (www.brunswickmusicfestival.com.au): the only inner-city festival in Australia celebrating traditional and contemporary acoustic music styles.

Australian International Airshow (www.airshow.net.au): held once every two years (2005, 2007 etc.), this is the biggest aviation and aerospace event in the Southern Hemisphere. Held at Avalon Airport near Geelong.

L'Oréal Melbourne Fashion Festival (www.mff.com.au): Australian fashion's public showcase.

April

The Melbourne International Comedy Festival (www.comedyfestival.com.au): one of the world's top three comedy festivals (after Edinburgh's Fringe and Montreal's Just for Laughs). Launched in 1987 by Barry Humphries and Peter Cook and still going strong, with shows all over the city.

The Melbourne International Flower and Garden Show (www.melbflowershow.com.au): held in Carlton Gardens and the Royal Exhibition Building, this is Australia's largest and most prestigious horticultural event, featuring spectacularly impressive floral displays.

May

St Kilda Film Festival (www.stkildafilmfestival.com.au): internationally recognised short film festival and competition.

July/August

Melbourne International Film Festival (www.melbournefilmfestival.com.au): showing the best feature films from Australia and around the world.

August

The Age Melbourne Writers' Festival (www.mwf.com.au): the foremost literary event of the year.

September

Melbourne Fringe Festival (www.melbournefringe.com.au): artists take over the streets of the city.

Royal Melbourne Show (www.royalshow.com.au): bringing the countryside to the city.

Autumn Moon Festival: Chinatown comes alive with colourful street decorations and entertainment.

October

Melbourne International Festival of the Arts (www.melbournefestival.com.au): one of the world's largest celebrations of arts, bringing the city streets to life with a wide range of local and international, indoor and outdoor, ticketed and free events.

Australian Motor Cycle Grand Prix: the premier event on the international motorcycle calendar, combining three World Championship races – 125cc, 250cc and the superstars of 500cc – staged at Victoria's spectacular Phillip Island circuit.

November

Melbourne Cup Carnival: unites people in a celebration of fashion (hats a high point), food and entertainment, culminating in the running of one of the world's most famous horse races, the Melbourne Cup.

December

Carols by Candlelight: outdoor carol singing in the days before Christmas at the Sidney Myer Music Bowl, King's Domain.

Right: national sport

Practical
Information

GETTING THERE

By Air

For the cheapest flights your best bet is to trawl the internet, or check out the advertisements in the travel pages of the Sunday supplements. Obviously, high season (November to March) is the most popular and expensive time to travel, and you should book your tickets well in advance.

Melbourne Airport (www.melbourne airport.com.au) is located 22 km (14 miles) northwest of the city along the Tullamarine Freeway and can easily be accessed by car, taxi or bus. Services at the airport include:

Exchange: There are four Thomas Cook foreign-exchange booths – two in arrivals and two in the departures – which are open daily to meet all arriving flights, from 5am–2am. ATMs are also available.

Accommodation and information: The Travellers' Information and Service Desk (tel: 9297 1805) on the ground floor of the International Terminal can book accommodation and help with general enquiries. Airport accommodation is available at the Holiday Inn opposite the terminal (tel: 9338 2322; www.ichotels group.com).

Shopping: Shops on the departure level of the International Terminal offer a wide range of products at guaranteed competitive prices. International travellers can pre-book their duty-free purchases by phone, tel: 8346 0888.

From the Airport

Taxis: There are numerous and efficient taxis outside all terminals. Expect to pay about $35–40 for the 30-minute trip into the centre of Melbourne.

Bus: SkyBus operates an efficient airport to city and return service approximately every half hour with several drop-off and pick-up points in the city. Tickets are available at the airport at a cost of $15 each way (tel: 9335 3066; www.skybus. com.au).

A number of bus services also link the airport with regional Victoria. Look up www.melbourne-airport.com.au for further details.

Car Rental: A selection of car-rental companies operate offices in the international domestic terminal as well as on the ground floor of the short-term car park. Among the major companies are:

Avis: tel: 9338 1800
www.avis.com
Budget: tel: 9338 6955
www.budget.com.au
Hertz: tel: 9338 4044
www.hertz.com
Thrifty: tel 9663 5200
www.thrifty.com.au

By Rail

The principal rail lines of Australia follow the east and south coasts, linking Melbourne to the other major cities of Cairns, Brisbane, Sydney and Adelaide. **V/Line** (tel: 139 196; www.vlinepassenger.com.au) operate rail services and a coach network.

By Road

The drive to Melbourne is interesting from whichever direction you approach. The route through the Australian Alps is rugged but spectacular, while the direct route from

Left: Bunjil, an eagle hawk, stands guard over the Docklands. **Right:** cool car

Sydney (along the Hume Highway) goes past some fine wineries in the historic north of Victoria. An alternative longer route from Sydney follows the coast via the Princes Highway, passing some excellent beaches. From Adelaide to the west, the famous drive along the Great Ocean Road includes some of Australia's most dramatic scenery, including the spectacular Twelve Apostles *(see pages 63–5)*.

By Sea

The only regular maritime connection with Melbourne is to and from Tasmania. The TT Line's *Spirit of Tasmania* is an overnight passenger and car ferry. Freecall **TT Line** on 1-800-030-344 for information (tel: 1800 634 906; www.spiritof-tasmania.com.au).

TRAVEL ESSENTIALS

Visas and Passports

All visitors to Australia, except citizens of Australia and New Zealand, need a visa or an **Electronic Travel Authority (ETA)**. An ETA is an electronically stored authorisation for tourist *(Visitor ETA)* or business *(Short Validity Business ETA)* entry. Both types allow for multiple visits begun within 12 months of issue (with a maxi-mum stay of three months per visit). This should be obtained prior to travel, through Australian visa offices or from travel agents or airlines (may charge). Or, for $20, enter your passport and credit card details online: www.eta.immi.gov.au.

Weather

Melbourne experiences four seasons (sometimes all in one day) and has a temperate climate. In summer, daytime temperatures average 25°C (77°F). In autumn and spring, daytime temperatures average 20°C (68°F) and 21°C (70°F) respectively, while in winter the average temperature is 14°C (57°F). The hottest months are normally January and February. The hottest Melbourne day on record was 13 January 1939, when the temperature reached 45.6°C (114°F).

Victoria has four distinct seasons:

Spring	September–November
Summer	December–February
Autumn	March–May
Winter	June–August

Temperatures vary across the state from the milder coastal regions and inland waterways to snow in winter in the Alpine snowfields just three hours by car from Melbourne. Snow occurs above 600 metres (1,950ft) between June and October.

USEFUL INFORMATION

Geography

Victoria is wedge shaped. Its greatest length, from east to west, is 794 km (498 miles) and its greatest breadth, from north to south, 467 km (294 miles). It is bounded on its southern coastline by the Southern Ocean, Bass Strait and the Pacific Ocean, and by the Murray River in the north. It shares a border with South Australia to the west and New South Wales to the north.

Population

Melbourne has a population of approximately 3.5 million, making it Australia's second-biggest city after Sydney. One in four Melburnians was born in another country. Melbourne has the third-largest Greek population of any city in the world and the most Italians in a city outside Italy.

MONEY MATTERS

Currency

Australia's currency uses the decimal system of dollars and cents (100 cents to the dollar). There are $100, $50, $20, $10 and $5 notes, gold-coloured $2 and $1 coins and 50, 20, 10 and 5 cent coins. There are no restrictions on importing currency or travellers' cheques but you cannot take more than $5,000 in cash out of Australia without prior approval. For up-to-date exchange rates, try www.x-rates.com.

Changing Money

Changing foreign currency or travellers' cheques is no problem at almost any bank. Normal banking hours are Mon–Thurs 9.30am–4pm and Fri 9.30am–5pm. The Bank of Melbourne is the only bank open on Saturday morning, 9am–noon. The Bank of Melbourne's central city branch is at 267 Collins Street (tel: 9654 1377). Banks are not open on Sundays or public holidays.

There are four Thomas Cook foreign-exchange booths at Melbourne Airport. Most of Melbourne's large hotels will also change currency or cheques, but the rate of exchange will be slightly lower than in a bank, as they charge a small commission.

There are also many foreign-exchange booths in the city centre. These have longer opening hours than banks, but their rates of exchange aren't as good. Try Interforex (next to the Grand Hyatt hotel), 109 Collins Street, Melbourne, open seven days a week 8am–8.40pm, tel: 9654 2768.

Melbourne's Climate			
Avge Max Temp (C/F)	Avge Min Temp (C/F)	Avge Rain (mm)	Avge Daily Hrs Sun
Jan	26/79	14/57	49.0	8.1
Feb	26/79	14/57	47.7	7.5
March	24/75	13/55	51.8	6.2
April	20/68	11/52	58.4	4.9
May	17/63	9/48	57.2	3.8
June	14/57	7/45	50.2	3.1
July	13/55	6/43	48.7	3.5
Aug	15/59	7/45	50.6	4.4
Sept	17/63	8/46	59.4	5.2
Oct	20/68	9/48	67.7	5.9
Nov	22/72	11/52	60.2	6.7
Dec	24/75	13/55	59.9	7.4

Left: Federation Square
Above: Brunswick Street blooms with life

Melbourne Metropoplitan Tram System

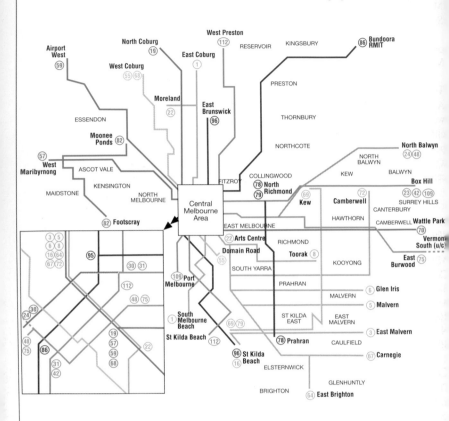

City Trams

Swanston Street
1 East Coburg-South Melbourne Beach
3 East Malvern
5 Malvern
6 Glen Iris
8 Toorak
16 St Kilda Beach
22 Moreland
64 East Brighton
67 Carnegie
72 Camberwell

Elizabeth Street
19 North Coburg
57 West Maribyrnong
59 Airport West
68 West Coburg
   (Sundays and Public Holidays only)

William Street
55 West Coburg-Domain Road (Mon-Sat)

La Trobe Street
24 North Balwyn
30 St Vincent's Plaza (Peak)

Bourke Street
86 Bundoora RMIT-Central Pier/Docklands
95 Melbourne Museum-Burke & Spencer Streets
96 St Kilda Beach-East Brunswick

Collins Street
112 West Preston-St Kilda
31 Spencer Street-Brunswick Street
42 Box Hill
109 Box Hill-Port Melbourne

Flinders Street
48 North Balwyn
75 East Burwood

Batman Avenue
70 Wattle Park

Suburban Trams
69 St Kilda Beach-Kew
78 Prahran-North Richmond
79 St Kilda Beach-North Richmond
82 Footscray-Moonee Ponds

Thomas Cook (tel: 9654 4222) has three foreign-exchange offices in Melbourne including one at 261 Bourke Street, open Mon–Fri 8.30am–5pm, Sat 9am– 4pm, Sun 10am–4pm.

American Express (tel: 9633 6333) has one city office at 233 Collins Street, open Mon–Fri 8.30am–5.30pm, Sat 9am–noon.

Travellers' Cheques

American Express, Thomas Cook and other well-known international brands of travellers' cheques are all widely used. A passport is adequate for identification, but it is a good idea to carry a driver's licence, credit card or a plane ticket in case of problems.

Australian dollar travellers' cheques are a good idea, as these can be exchanged without being converted into a foreign currency and incurring commission fees.

Major banks include:

Commonwealth Bank
385 Bourke Street, tel: 9675 7000.
ANZ Bank
100 Queen Street, tel: 9273 5555.
National Bank
500 Bourke Street, tel: 8641 3500.

Credit Cards

The most commonly accepted credit cards in Victoria are Visa, MasterCard, American Express and Bankcard.

With the advent of electronic banking and ATMs, a debit or credit card can be the ideal way to organise your money for travelling. Visa, MasterCard and American Express cards are commonly accepted in ATMs. Cash advances are also available over the counter from all banks.

Tax Refund Scheme

Under the Tourist Refund Scheme (TRS) both GST (Goods and Services Tax, 9 percent) and WET (Wine Equalisation Tax, 4.5 percent) can be collected before leaving Australia, although this only applies to purchases taken out as hand luggage. For further information, tel: 1300 363 263; www. customs.gov.au).

Right: a city-bound tram

GETTING AROUND

Trams

Melbourne's tram and light rail network, the largest outside Europe, makes travelling round the city cheap and convenient.

To ride Melbourne's trams you need to pre-purchase short-trip, two-hour, daily, weekly, monthly or yearly travel cards which are validated in machines on board. Pre-purchase tickets are available from the Met Shop (103 Elizabeth Street or visit www.victrip.com.au) in the city or a variety of city and suburban outlets, including newsagents and convenience stores. Short trip and two-hour tickets can be purchased from machines on board, but you will need coins. Tickets can be used on Melbourne's tram, rail and bus networks.

City Circle tram service

The City Circle tram, a free hop-on hop-off service running around the city, is an excellent way for tourists to explore the city. It takes passengers past many of the major attractions and has been extended to include the Docklands area. Information leaflets and maps are available free on board each tram. For the route, visit www.metlinkmelbourne.com.au.

Trams run in both directions every 10 minutes, from 10am–6pm (except Christmas Day and Good Friday). The service

practical information

extends its hours to 9pm during the months of daylight saving (late October to late March) on Thursday, Friday and Saturday.

Trains and buses

Melbourne also operates an extensive train and bus network in the city and suburbs. For bus routes and suburban and city train information, tel: 131 638. For information on all public transport, call the Transport Information Centre, tel: 9617 0900.

Bicycle Hire

Melbourne is a great cycling city, with kilometres of cycle tracks along the Yarra River and beyond.

Hire a Bike

Yarra River Bank (south side), below Princes Bridge, tel: 0417 339 203.

Borsari Cycles

193 Lygon Street, Carlton, tel: 9347 4100.
St Kilda Cycles
11 Carlisle Street, St Kilda, tel: 9534 3074.

HOURS & HOLIDAYS

Business hours:
Mon–Fri 9am–5pm.

City shopping hours
Mon–Wed 9am–5.30pm, Thurs 9am–7pm, Fri 9am–9pm, Sat and Sun 9am–5pm.

Public Holidays

New Year's Day – 1 Jan
Australia Day – 26 Jan
Labour Day (Victoria) – early Mar
Good Friday – late Mar/early Apr
Easter Monday – late Mar/early Apr
Anzac Day – 25 Apr
Queen's Birthday – 14 Jun
Melbourne Cup – 1st Tues in Nov
Christmas Day – 25 Dec
Boxing Day – 26 Dec

ACCOMMODATION

Melbourne has a good selection of accommodation in all price ranges. Many of the top hotels have first-class business facilities. The following is a list of selected accommodation divided into four price categories:

> **$$$$** – $400 and over
> **$$$** – $250–$400
> **$$** – $150–$250
> **$** – under $150

Price categories are for a standard double room, although in the budget category ($) many are for a bed in a shared dormitory or basic single room *(see page 89)*.

Hotel Como

630 Chapel Street, South Yarra
Tel: 9825 2222; fax: 9824 1263
www.mirvachotels.com.au
A five-star hotel whose accommodation options include spas, private Japanese garden, fully equipped kitchens, balconies, one- or two-bedroom suites or a private office fitted out with personal computer, printer, modem and fax machine. Spas in most suites and studios, king-size beds, combination safes in each suite and a voice-mail facility on all telephone extensions. There is an all-weather chlorinated salt-water pool with retractable glass roof, a gymnasium, spa and sauna. **$$$$**

Crown Towers Hotel

9 Whiteman Street, Southbank
Tel: 9292 6666; fax: 9292 6600
www.crowntowers.com.au

Left: Crown Towers Hotel, Southbank

Located on the southern bank of the Yarra River in the Crown Entertainment Complex *(see page 58)*, this is the place to stay if you like your nightlife on tap; there are cinemas, nightclubs, bars, restaurants, an indoor theme park, the luxurious Crown Spa and of course the Crown Casino. The bedrooms are spacious, with huge bathrooms, but the best thing about them is that they all have spectacular views of the city or Port Phillip Bay. $$$$

Park Hyatt
1 Parliament Square
(off Parliament Place), City
Tel: 9224 1234; fax: 9224 1200
www.melbourne.park.hyatt.com
Opposite St Patrick's Cathedral, this hotel is designed as a haven of luxury, relaxation and comfort. It has 240 spacious guest rooms and suites. Located in one of the city's treasured historic precincts, the hotel is bordered by grand old elm trees and the verdant Fitzroy Gardens. Hotel facilities include a bistro, bar, tea lounge, restaurant, cigar bar, ballroom and supporting function facilities, health club and spa. $$$$

Sheraton Towers Southgate
1 Southgate Avenue, Southbank
Tel: 9696 3100; fax: 9690 5889
A choice of 385 beautifully appointed rooms including 11 luxurious executive suites and a presidential suite. Has good business facilities, catering for meetings and functions numbering from six to 360 guests. The spacious rooms feature king-size beds, large windows, executive desks, wing-side armchairs and ottomans and marble bathrooms. $$$$

Hotel Sofitel
25 Collins Street, City
Tel: 9653 0000; fax: 9653 04261
www.sofitelmelbourne.com.au
Located at the Paris end of Collins Street in the heart of the central business district. Accommodation starts on level 36 with 363 guest rooms, including 52 suites offering stunning floor-to-ceiling panoramic views over Melbourne. Featuring the multi-award winning Le Restaurant, there is exceptional dining to suit all tastes. The hotel also features a ballroom, conference facilities, auditorium, two bars and a health and fitness club. $$$$

All Seasons
Welcome Hotel Melbourne
265–281 Little Bourke Street, City
Tel: 9639 0555; fax: 9639 1179
www.accorhotels.com.au
Located in the centre of the theatre and shopping district, and well known for its friendly staff, professional service and comprehensive facilities, which include: 24-hour reception, theatre/airline ticket bookings, guest laundry room, complimentary use of Melbourne City Baths/Gym, conference and function facilities for up to 150 people, plus the Seasons Restaurant, and bar, Ong international food court and room service. $$$

Hilton International
Melbourne Airport
Arrival Drive, PO Box 5042
Melbourne Airport
Tel: 8336 2000; fax: 8336 2001
www.hilton.com
Convenient airport accommodation, with direct access to both the international and domestic terminals via covered walkways. Restaurant and health club, with pool, spa and sauna. $$$

Hotel Lindrum
26 Flinders Street, City
Tel: 9668 1111; fax: 9668 1189
www.hotellindrum.com.au
Located in an historic building in the heart of Melbourne, and minutes away from theatres, restaurants, boutiques, shopping centres and major sporting venues such as the Melbourne Cricket Ground. The hotel has 59 spacious rooms and suites complete with CD/stereo systems, fax and modem points. There's a boardroom for business meetings. On the ground floor, guests can enjoy gourmet cuisine. $$$

Novotel Melbourne on Collins
270 Collins Street, City
Tel: 9650 5800; fax: 9650 7100
www.accorhotels.com.au
Overlooks the spectacular atrium of the prestigious Australia on Collins shopping centre. 323 rooms, 37 studios and five meeting rooms that can hold up to 300 delegates. The hotel facilities include indoor heated swimming pool, sauna, spa pool and gym. Guest facilities include 24-hour reception, 24-hour room service, laundry and dry-cleaning service, concierge, tour/airline and car rental coordination. $$$

Quay West Hotel
Southgate Boulevard, Southbank
Tel: 9693 6000
www.mirvachotels.com.au
Quay West Hotel is located in the heart of Southgate precinct on the banks of the Yarra River, close to shops, restaurants and bars, and adjacent to the Victorian Arts Centre and the National Gallery of Victoria. The all-suite property has 172 luxurious one- and two-bedroom suites and five-star hotel services and facilities. $$$

The Westin Melbourne
Regent Place
205 Collins Street, City
Tel: 03 9626 4146
www.starwood.com/westin
A new inner-city hotel in an outstanding location, with easy access to prime shopping, theatres and restaurants. The hotel has 125 rooms, some with balconies overlooking Melbourne's City Square, 13 luxury suites, a presidential suite and 18 serviced apartments, along with a Wellness Centre with swimming pool, spa, gym and steam room. Also offers a speciality food court, Mediterranean restaurant and all day brasserie-style restaurant. $$$

The Windsor
103 Spring Street, City
Tel: 9633 6000; fax: 9633 6001
www.thewindsor.com.au
The Windsor, built in 1883, is one of the world's great romantic hotels. A Victorian Heritage Hotel, it was fully restored in the early 1980s. In-room facilities include: the latest-release video movies, CNN, direct-dial telephone and fax, voice mail, modem outlet, bathrobes, hair dryers and personal mini bar. $$$

Batman's Hill Hotel
66–70 Spencer Street, City
Tel: 9614 6344; fax: 9614 1189
www.batmanshill.com.au
Steps away is the Melbourne Convention and Exhibition Centre, as well as the Crown Casino and Entertainment Complex. The hotel has a 24-hour reception, room service, babysitting, valet and dry-cleaning services. Fax and photocopying services. $$

Explorers Inn Hotel
16 Spencer Street, City
Tel: 9621 3333
www.explorerinns.com.au
Situated in the central business district opposite Melbourne Exhibition and Convention Centre and Crown Casino, this hotel offers 93 rooms with friendly and personalised service. $$

Hotel Ibis Melbourne
12–21 Therry Street, City
Tel: 9639 2399; fax: 9639 1988
www.ibishotel.com

Above: the Windsor Hotel is a romantic place

Hotel Ibis has 250 rooms, one- and two-bedroom apartments and split-level two-bedroom apartments each with reverse cycle air conditioning. All apartments have a kitchenette, separate lounge with divan and bathroom. In the heart of Melbourne, the hotel also offers a restaurant and bar, and convention areas. $$

Metropole Hotel Apartments
44 Brunswick Street, Fitzroy
Tel: 9411 8100
Fax: 9411 8200
www.metropole.org
The Metropole's convenient location allows visitors to sample the liveliness of Brunswick Street, Johnston Street and the surrounding areas. The property consists of 60 self-contained apartments and studios, conference and meeting facilities. The units are ideal for families and longer-stay travellers. $$

Somerset Botanic Gardens
348 St Kilda Road
Tel: 9685 3000
Fax: 9685 2999
www.the-ascott.com
Situated on one of Melbourne's most gracious boulevards, this hotel is within easy reach of the city and is the perfect business base with personal computer facilities, fax lines and meeting and function rooms. Smartly furnished and extremely comfortable, the hotel specialises in spacious living and dining areas, fully equipped kitchens, and a health club that has a 12-metre (39-ft) lap pool – perfect for unwinding at the end of the day. $$

Budget Accommodation $
The list of budget accommodation that follows includes hostels. Many establishments have dormitory rooms as well as single and double rooms, so be sure to clarify what you require. Dorm rooms range from $15 to $28, while doubles run from $45 to $86. In addition, there are all kinds of permutations of twin, triple and even single rooms.

The City & North Melbourne area
Hotel Bakpak
167 Franklin Street, City
Tel: 9329 7525
www.bakpakgroup.com

Exford Hotel
199 Russell Street, City
Tel: 9663 2697
www.exfordhotel.com.au

The Friendly Backpacker
197 King Street, City
Tel: 9670 1111
www.friendlygroup.com.au

Global Backpackers
238 Victoria Street, North Melbourne
Tel: 9328 3728

Gunn Island Hotel
102 Canterbury Road
Middle Park
Tel: 9690 1958
www.gunnisland.com.au

Homestay Victoria
Level 10, 118 Queen Street, City
Tel: 9642 1566
An accommodation placement service providing rooms for overseas students with Australian families.

Kingsgate Hotel
131 King Street, City
Tel: 9629 4171
www.kingsgatehotel.com.au

Melbourne Metro
78 Howard Street, North Melbourne
Tel: 9329 8599
www.yha.com.au
Run by the Youth Hostel Association. Winner of tourism award in 2003.

Melbourne Oasis YHA
76 Chapman Street, North Melbourne
Tel: 9328 3595
www.yha.com.au

The Nunnery
116 Nicholson Street, Fitzroy
Tel: 1800 032 635 or 9419 8637
www.bakpakgroup.com/nunnery

The Spencer
475 Spencer Street, City
Tel: 9329 7755
www.hotelspencer.com

Toad Hall Hotel
441 Elizabeth Street, City
Tel: 9600 9010
www.toadhallhotel.com.au

Hotel Y
489 Elizabeth Street, City
Tel: 8327 2760
www.ywca.net
Women only.

St Kilda Area
Base Backpackers
17 Carlisle Street
Tel: 8598 6204
www.basebackpackers.com
State-of-the-art hostel featuring an up-market girls-only level and a hip bar.

Bayside Motel
63 Fitzroy St
Tel: 9525 3833

Chapel Street Backpackers
24 Grey Street, Windsor

Tel: 9533 6855
www.csbackpackers.com.au
En-suite rooms are available for a few dollars extra.

Coffee Palace
24 Grey Street
Tel: 9534 5283

Olembia Beachside
96 Barkly Street
Tel: 9537 1412
www.olembia.com.au

Oslo Hotel for Backpackers
38 Grey Street
Tel: 9525 4498
www.oslohotel.com.au

The Ritz Backpackers
169 Fitzroy Street
Tel: 9525 3501
www.backpackerscentre.com

Other Areas
Lords Lodge
204 Punt Road, South Yarra
Tel: 9510 5658
www.lordslodge.com.au

Market Inn
143 York Street,
South Melbourne
Tel: 9690 2220
www.marketinn.com.au

Richmond Hill Guest House
353 Church Street, Richmond
Tel: 9428 6501
www.richmondhillhotel.com.au

EMERGENCIES

Medical treatment in Australia can be expensive, so visitors are strongly advised to take out a comprehensive insurance policy before leaving home. The only exception to this rule is visitors from New Zealand, who are covered by the Australian national health scheme (known as Medicare).

Vaccinations are not necessary if you fly direct to Australia and have not passed through an epidemic zone or a smallpox, typhoid, yellow fever or cholera zone in the preceding 14 days.

Hospitals
The Alfred
Commercial Road, Prahran
Tel: 9276 2000

Royal Melbourne
Grattan Street, Parkville
Tel: 9342 7000

St Vincent's
41 Victoria Parade, Fitzroy
Tel: 9288 2211

The Traveller's Medical and Vaccination Centre
2nd Floor, 393 Little Bourke Street
Tel: 9602 5788
www.traveldoctor.com.au
Open Mon–Fri 8.30am–5.30pm, Sat 9am–noon

24-Hour Emergency Numbers
Fire, tel: 000
Police, tel: 000
Ambulance, tel: 000
Lifeline Counselling Service
Tel: 131 114
Poisons Information Service
Tel: 131 126

POST & TELECOMMUNICATIONS

Telephoning
The Melbourne area code is 03. The code for Australia is 61, so when dialling from overseas, dial 00 61 3, followed by the number. Local calls from public telephones in Australia cost a flat rate of $0.40 – local calls in Australia are not timed. Most public telephones in Australia use pre-paid phone cards, available from post offices, newsagents, gift shops and many other outlets in denominations from $5 to $50. These can be used to make local, interstate and international calls.

Calling Overseas
International Direct Dial (IDD) telephone calls can be made from most public telephones. Dial the international access code (0011), then the country code, the area code (omitting any initial zero) and the telephone number.

Telephoning Interpreting Service
A free 24-hour service offering assistance in communication in over 100 languages. To access, tel: 131 450.

Mobile Phones
It is possible to hire a mobile phone from Vodaphone Rental at Melbourne Airport, Street Level, International Arrivals (tel: 9335 4455; www.vodafonerental.com.au).

Postal Services
Post offices are open Mon–Fri 9am–5pm. They will hold mail for visitors (address it to Poste Restante at the nearest post office to your accommodation).

Internet Cafés
Global Chat
22 Elizabeth Street
Tel: 9654 3666
Hipper Lounge.com
Mid Level M21, Southgate
Tel: 9690 3099
Kinko's 136 Exhibition Street
Tel: 9650 3588

USEFUL ADDRESSES

Melbourne Visitor Information Centre

Corner Flinders Street and St Kilda Road, Federation Square; tel: 9658 9658; fax: 9650 6168; www.visit melbourne.com. Open 9am–6pm.

Look for the sign of the distinctive yellow 'i' against a blue background. This was the first multimedia, multilingual visitor centre in Australia, providing orientation and information on attractions, events, activities and internet access, and an accommodation and tour booking service. Visitor information is available in six languages – English, Cantonese, German, Japanese, Korean and Mandarin.

Melbourne Greeter Service

Based at the Visitor Information Centre above, this service offers visitors the opportunity to meet an enthusiastic volunteer who will take them on a free one-on-one orientation tour of the city. Visitors are matched with volunteer 'greeters' according to language and shared interests. Speakers of more than 30 languages are available. Bookings are essential (a minimum of three days notice is required).

City Ambassadors

Melbourne's award-winning city ambassadors are another good source of city information. Dressed in distinctive red uniforms, the ambassadors rove the retail heart of the city, dispensing directions or simply lending visitors a hand.

Victorian Tourism Information Service

Tel: 132 842; www.visitvictoria.com
Provides general information on Victoria and its attractions.

Disabled services

NICAN (**National Information Communication Awareness Network**) provides a free information service for people with disabilities. Freecall/TTY: 1800 806 769; tel: 02 6285 3713; email: info@nican.com.au.

FURTHER READING

Other Insight Guides

Insight Guide: Australia. Extensively revised, with new maps, photographs and Travel Tips.

Insight Pocket Guide: Sydney. Tailormade itineraries, ideal if you are pressed for time.

General

Australian Dreaming: 40,000 Years of Aboriginal History. Compiled and edited by Jennifer Isaacs. Sydney: Lansdowne Press.

The Heritage of Australia: The Illustrated Register of the National Estate. Melbourne: Macmillan.

Wilderness Australia by David McGonigal. Sydney: Reed Books.

Australian Geographic Book of the Kimberley by David McGonigal. Sydney: Australian Geographic.

A Land Half Won. Melbourne: Macmillan.

The Tyranny of Distance by Geoffrey Blainey. Penguin Australia.

The Fatal Shore by Robert Hughes. New York: Vintage Books. The classic account of the convict system.

The Other Side of the Frontier by Henry Reynolds. Penguin Australia. An account of colonial settlement from the Aboriginal point of view.

Above: hitting the beat

ART & PHOTO CREDITS

1, 2/3, 8/9, 28, 30, 31, 32T/B, 35, 41B, 45, 51, 58, 67, 71, 80, 90	**Jerry Dennis**
5B, 6T/B, 7T/B, 23B, 25T, 26T/B, 38T/B, 39, 40, 43, 47, 48, 50, 52B, 53, 55, 69, 73, 75, 76, 81, 83, 85, 88, 92	**Andrew Tauber/Apa**
23T	**Melbourne Aquarium**
11, 13, 15	**State Library of Victoria**
12, 14T/B, 16, 24, 27, 66, 72	**Coo-ee Hictorical Picture Library**
20, 21, 25B, 33, 34, 37, 42, 44, 49, 52T, 56, 59, 61, 64B, 65, 68, 74, 77, 78, 82, 86	**Tourism Victoria Photographic Library**
29, 36	**Ben Swinnerton**
57	**Queen Victoria Market Pty**
41T	**C.M. Thomas**
60, 62	**Peter Lalor**
63	**Mark Read**
79	**Glyn Genin**
64T	**Julie Mason**
70	**Tony Perrottet**
54	**Simon Bayliss/Tourism Victoria Photographic Library**
Cover	**Corbis**
Back Cover	**Tourism Victoria & Andrew Tauber**
Cover Design	**Klaus Geisler**
Cartography	**Berndston & Berndston**

index

INDEX

Limerick
County Library